AIKI-JUJUTSU

MIXED MARTIAL ART
OF THE SAMURAI

AIKI-JUJUTSU

MIXED MARTIAL ART
OF THE SAMURAI

CARY NEMEROFF

THE CROWOOD PRESS

First published in 2013 by
The Crowood Press Ltd
Ramsbury, Marlborough
Wiltshire SN8 2HR

www.crowood.com

British Library Cataloguing-in-Publication Data
A catalogue record for this book is available from the British Library.

ISBN 978 1 84797 478 5

Typeset by Jean Cussons Typesetting, Diss, Norfolk

Printed and bound in India by Replika Press

CONTENTS

CONTENTS

AUTHOR'S BIOGRAPHY

Cary Nemeroff, author of *Mastering the Samurai Sword* (Singapore: Tuttle Publishing, 2008), is a teacher of the Okinawan and Japanese martial arts, who has merged his interests in education, individuals with disabilities and the Asian combat arts into a full-time career. He has earned a Bachelor of Arts degree in Philosophy from New York University, as well as a Master of Arts degree in Education from Teachers College, Columbia University, New York.

Cary's martial arts training began as a young boy in 1977 under the auspices of Juko-Kai International, a martial arts organization accredited in both Okinawa and the mainland of Japan. As an adolescent, his passion and skills as a martial artist grew and he ultimately became the personal student of Dr Rod Sacharnoski, President of Juko-Kai International. This relationship continues to this day. Cary has earned a 10th Degree Black Belt in Aiki-Jujutsu (Jujutsu), as well as a 9th Degree Black Belt in a variety of other Okinawan and Japanese martial arts.

Cary is founder and president of Fukasa-Ryu Bujutsu Kai, a martial arts organization that is a member of the International Okinawan Martial Arts Union and is accredited and sponsored by the Zen Kokusai Soke Budo/Bugei Renmei.

At present, Cary conducts an extensive programme of group classes for adults and children at the JCC in Manhattan, a state-of-the-art fitness and cultural facility located on the Upper West Side of New York City. Cary is fluent in sign language and conducts specialized classes for children and adults with physical and cognitive challenges, including autism and cerebral palsy. Among the martial arts he teaches are Aiki-Jujutsu, the Samurai sword (Iai-Jutsu and Ken-Jutsu), Karate and Toide (Okinawan throwing and grappling). At other venues, such as United Cerebral Palsy of NYC, he designs customized programmes and provides staff training, individual instruction and conducts clinics for schools affiliated with his own organization.

Cary Nemeroff can be reached through the Fukasa Kai website (www.fukasakai.com).

FOREWORD

Aiki-Jujutsu is the art of the Bushi, leaders of the class of Japanese warriors known as the Samurai. It was originally developed as a method to overcome sword-wielding assailants on the battlefield and, like most Japanese arts, it developed into an outstanding form of self-defence that could be utilized in modern times. I have been involved in the Japanese Jujutsu arts most of my life and have studied the Bushi warrior skill at its highest level.

Aiki is the skill to harmonize with an attacker in order to overcome one's difference in size, strength or fighting ability. When people can actually 'Aiki' their opponents, they can neutralize and overcome them. Many of the traditional Japanese styles have developed the concept of Aiki to an incredible level. Having studied several of these martial styles, I have developed my own form of Juko-Ryu Aiki-Jujutsu, which preserves these powerful techniques for modern-day combat and self-defence.

Cary Nemeroff has been my student for more than thirty-five years. I am pleased to recommend his book on Aiki-Jujutsu to those who are interested in the traditional martial arts of Japan. Aiki-Jujutsu is one of the most magnificent martial arts that came from the Japanese tradition. Anyone interested in traditional training with a strong self-defence component will find this book interesting and instructive.

Rod Sacharnoski, Soke, 10th Dan
Headmaster, Juko-Ryu Bujutsu-Kai
9th Dan Hanshi, Seidokan Okinawa

ACKNOWLEDGEMENTS

I would like to acknowledge all of the people who helped bring this text to completion. First and foremost, I want to thank my mother, Sandy Nemeroff, for her role in editing the text in the manuscript. Her words helped the conversion of martial arts techniques into meaningful language.

I thank both of my parents for enrolling me in the martial arts as a young boy. Their persistence and constant encouragement throughout my life continue to give me the confidence to pursue my dreams.

I am grateful for my wife Tsen-Ting, my partner in life, who understands and appreciates the lifestyle that I live, which is inextricably connected to the commitment that I have to the martial arts.

I would like to honour my teacher, Rod Sacharnoski, Soke, who continues to inspire me through his philosophy and mastery of martial arts techniques. It is his generosity, trust and patience that has sculpted me into the martial artist that I am today. I am honoured that he would, once again, write the Foreword for my book.

Many thanks to all the devoted students who contributed through the photographs in the book: David Nemeroff, Dai-Shihan; Kevin Ng, Shihan; Greg Zenon, Shihan-Dai; Nicolas Fulton, Shihan-Dai; Anthony Cabrera, Sensei; Ittai Korin, Sensei; David Schnier, Sensei; Bret Koppin, Sensei; Peter Lawson, Sensei; Anita V. Stockett, Sensei; Fred Bennett, Sensei; Frantz Cochy and Wade Bailey. I am honoured by and grateful for their belief in me and my teachings, as well as their demonstration of diligence and commitment to what I do.

To Greg Zenon, Shihan-Dai, the 'Fukasa-Kai Photographer' who photographed 99 per cent of the fabulous pictures in this publication, I want to share my special thanks for all of his photographic contributions during the last fifteen years as a member of Fukasa-Kai.

To David Nemeroff, Dai-Shihan, who photographed the cover picture for this publication, I want to share my deepest thanks for all of his hard work and support to help Fukasa-Kai evolve to where it is today.

I wish to thank all of my devoted students. Without them, my life would be far less satisfying.

PART I

MARTIAL HISTORY

The traditional martial arts of Japan have survived the test of time. Martial history provides us with evidence that Bujutsu (the Japanese martial arts) proliferated and evolved over generations within the small families of Samurai who, beginning in Japan's Heian period (794–1185CE), served both their Daimyo (regional lords) and ultimately the emperor and/or Shogun (military leader). Martial arts techniques were tested on the battlefields, where soldiers collided in cavalry battles as foot soldiers *en masse* and in individual bouts. A Samurai's brazenness and martial aptitude were tested, resulting in either the death of one of the combatants or *Seppuku* (ritual suicide to preserve one's honour).

CHAPTER I

BUJUTSU: MARTIAL ARTS

The knowledge that a Samurai derived, and reflected upon, from his experiences in battle enabled him to formulate a methodology and breadth of technique. This 'system' or Ryu represented a unique school of thought or style. A Ryu would typically be taught or 'passed down' to the progeny of the Samurai, who would serve Japan later in life.

The Samurai, who devoted their lives to serving their country, trained in and developed a full spectrum of martial arts techniques that were effective in many different battle contexts. This complete fighting system would have been practised with the objective of perfecting the Samurai's techniques. A period of reflection subsequent to combat could have led to the inclusion of additional forms.

Power changed hands fairly rapidly throughout the history of Japan. The country endured chaotic periods of warfare and disharmony as emperors attempted to exercise authority, while clans of militants usurped power and control of Japan's resources. This reality led to the proliferation of 'battle-ready' Samurai poised for imminent engagement.

The beginning of the seventeenth century marked a noticeable change, as Japan became stable for approximately 250 years under the leadership of the Tokugawa Family (Edo period: 1603–1868CE). The small island of Okinawa represented the only significant conquest for territorial expansion during this era. Its annexation was a successful, swift operation, occurring just subsequent to the beginning of the Tokugawas' reign. In Japan, this period of 'relative' peace drastically changed the day-to-day duties of the previously warring Samurai to more of a policing role, the purpose of which was to uphold order and execute the wishes of the Tokugawas. This circumstance represented an important turn-ing point in the evolution of the Samurai martial arts; it was a time of profound reflection and martial arts practice outside the context of battlefield warfare. In this new era, a Samurai would have been more likely to have found himself involved in a one-on-one bout in plain clothes, as opposed to the typical armour worn by a field soldier. Such a change had a major impact upon how martial arts techniques could be used; for example, a Samurai confronted by an adversary wearing armour would have been limited to using striking techniques that could penetrate only the open areas in the opponent's armour. These vulnerable areas, usually located around the joints of the body, were under-protected to allow for unobstructed movement. Faced with an 'armour-free' opponent, however, a Samurai could have been virtually limitless in his ability to strike any part of his opponent's body. Furthermore, if the Samurai himself were wearing plain clothing, the rigid layers of armour that could have otherwise hampered his ability to protect himself would no longer be an issue, as he would now be able to move his body freely, without the obstruction caused by rigid armour. The Samurai arts evolved further through the integration of the wisdom acquired by the forefathers of past generations, 'the battlefield warriors', into a more holistic lifestyle consisting of reflection, enlightenment via rigorous training, meditation and the occasional bout that enabled the Samurai to carry out his duty to Japan and to obtain martial acuity and experience through real confrontation.

Soon after the fall of the Tokugawa Dynasty, Emperor Meiji allowed for the set-up of a government comprised of a council of Japanese officials, who would decide on laws that would be enforced by police-like figures. In 1876, the Samurai, who typically served in this capacity, were stripped of this honour and their privilege to carry a Katana (a long Samurai sword) in public. The new decrees ended a tradition that would survive on in small families of Samurai who perceived the value of the Samurai lifestyle to be its balance between physical prowess and spiritual enlightenment. Contemporary life brought about great change to the martial arts of the Samurai. There were, however, individuals who made a valiant effort to preserve and protect the Koryu, the ancient martial arts of the Samurai, so the lessons acquired from real combat would not face extinction.

Ryu: Style or System 'School of Thought'

The Meiji Era (1868–1912) changed the manner in which most Samurai lived their lives. The new government disregarded the Samurai's skills as great fighters and defenders of Japan's honour. Stipends, previously paid to Samurai for their service to Japan, became a thing of the past. Swordsmen also found themselves without work, because Japan was now importing modern instruments of war (such as guns). In many cases, swordsmen took on other crafts, such as the construction of horseshoes, to which they could apply their skills. The Samurai, however, most often refused to accept the disgrace of taking on jobs for the sake of supporting themselves and their families. Some Samurai committed Seppuku, thereby manifesting a preference to die an 'honourable' death in lieu of declining into what they perceived to be a sub-standard socioeconomic class.

For those who valued the Samurai traditions of their forefathers, there was hope for a future for the many martial Ryu that had been constructed of techniques capable of addressing the full spectrum of combat inevitabilities. In an effort to preserve the many lessons learned during battle, martial Ryu would be documented by an accounting or logging of techniques.

Martial Ryu techniques were classified in several ways. Some were characterized as emanating from a particular position, i.e. stationary, moving, seated,

kneeling or lying. Techniques could also be sub-categorized into fist, foot, throwing and grappling methods, any of which may or may not have been used in tandem with weapons. As the practitioners of a particular Ryu classified and systematized their techniques into individual categories, the martial arts began to take the shape of separate disciplines, each falling under a quintessential, philosophical umbrella and methodology. After the techniques of a Ryu were documented and then classified into distinct martial arts categories, a martial Ryu or unique methodology became bona fide and would be recognized by others as an autonomous entity.

It should be the case that the more time a Ryu, composed of individual arts, had to evolve, the greater would be the breadth of techniques under its umbrella. The martial Ryu that proliferated during early Samurai times survived many generations by being passed down within Samurai families. These Ryu, known as Koryu, represent the greatest number of martial arts disciplines unified under any distinct Ryu. Having developed prior to the Meiji Era, the traditional Japanese martial Ryu referred to as Kobudo (ancient martial ways) tended to be comprised of just one or a few martial arts and did not evolve over the course of many generations of Samurai service. As I mentioned earlier, during the relatively peaceful Edo period, the Samurai, unlike their predecessors, served as patrolmen as opposed to fighters on battlefields. While this might have resulted in the development of fewer new techniques during this period, I surmise that the Samurai made great efforts to preserve and practise the techniques and strategies of their forefathers. Modifications of old martial arts techniques were probably retrofitted to accommodate the new circumstances in which the Samurai now found themselves.

A 'career' Samurai's life centred upon the study of all of the techniques of a Ryu. When the Samurai's duty to Japan became defunct, however, he had to split his time between his martial study and practice, and his other occupational responsibilities. Within the course of his life, the Samurai now had less time to develop his martial ability and fewer opportunities in which to use his skill to fend off a real attack. The separation and classification of groups of techniques into different categories and individual martial arts afforded a part-time practitioner a greater chance of mastering all the techniques of a particular class during his lifetime.

Individuals today who have creatively integrated the martial arts into a full-time career can live the holistic lifestyle of the martial arts by practising and sharing it with others who see the value in the discipline and lifestyle. Others may choose to utilize martial arts techniques in contemporary law enforcement and the security professions. While the latter can be a great forum in which to test one's skill, regular 'off the job' training must be maintained for martial acuity and to keep the body fit for optimal performance.

The Individual Martial Arts Disciplines

The oldest martial arts of the Samurai developed around a primary weapon, the Samurai sword. Ken-Jutsu, techniques in the unsheathed use of the sword, focused on every aspect of blade offence and defence, from cutting, thrusting and blocking to the strategy and practice of fencing. Other auxiliary weapons, such as the Naginata (glaive), Yari (spear) and Tanto (knife), modelled their techniques after Ken-Jutsu. The weapons-free martial arts employed by the Samurai also evolved from the manner in which the Samurai sword was used. These techniques were developed for occasions of an 'emergency nature', such as when a Samurai's sword became non-functional during battle due to damage to the weapon.

The techniques of the weapons-free art of Aiki-Jujutsu, or simply Jujutsu, were designed to counter attacks against a Samurai sword-wielding opponent by use of evasive blocking, striking, disarming, throwing and grappling techniques; and in every phase of defence, a connection to the strategy, movements, cuts and blocks of the Samurai sword arts is manifested. These techniques were systematized into an effective, weapons-free martial art. Aiki-Jujutsu is comprised of many elements and is often referred to as the 'grandfather' of the Japanese Samurai weapons-free martial arts. Aiki-Jujutsu can be depicted in a hierarchy that includes all the arts that proliferated from it and is separated into three elements, which are characterized by the type of technique and context in which the particular technique could be applied by the Samurai. The elements to which I am alluding are now known as the following martial arts: Kempo-Jutsu, Aiki-Jutsu and Ju-Jutsu (the less comprehensive version). While it might appear that mastery of the techniques of each element or martial arts discipline would lead to a complete understanding of Aiki-Jujutsu, it is my contention that the 'whole is greater than the sum of its parts'. Let us take a closer look at the Samurai martial art of Aiki-Jujutsu in the way that contemporaries dissected it.

Ken-Jutsu.

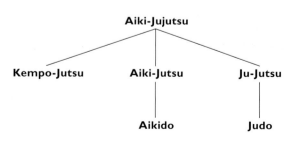

Japanese weapons-free martial arts hierarchy.

Kempo-Jutsu

This weapons-free martial art translates as 'fist law' and is the first mode of defence dictating evasive and retaliatory strikes to an opponent. In addition to a safe evasion, Kempo-Jutsu should position the body within adequate range of an opponent in order to use an effective retaliatory strike and possible follow-up (an Aiki-Jujutsu throwing or joint-locking technique). While Kempo-Jutsu has a symbiotic relationship with Aiki-Jutsu and Ju-Jutsu, it can be used alone. On its own, it is a martial art comprised almost entirely of blocks, strikes, and evasive and invasive movements. The strong strategic tactical element of the art provides for efficiency of movement, powerful strikes and the quick execution of follow-up techniques. This is why I characterize it as a most critical first method of defence for the unarmed Samurai.

In the more advanced levels of Kempo-Jutsu, the student is taught to direct strikes toward the more 'sensitive' areas of the human body in a quick, explosive manner. These 'precision' strikes were designed to penetrate the unprotected or lightly protected joint areas of the body that were not covered by heavy Samurai armour. These areas were similar to the targets used by the sword-wielding Samurai.

Almost every part of the hand can be used to strike targets, such as an opponent's eyes, throat, ears, armpits, groin, ribs and so on. The martial art's complex hand-shapes are intricately similar to the way in which one 'finger spells' in sign language. These hand-shapes, capable of cutting through the air at speeds much greater than the tightened fist could ever travel, are strengthened by the tightening of the hand and bending of the fingers and thumb just prior to impact. While Kempo-Jutsu does utilize the fist in its arsenal of strikes, the 'precision strikes' are used to spear, clip, slash and hook an opponent's vital areas in a debilitating and sometimes lethal way. (Since this book is focused on the fundamental techniques of the art, I will not elaborate upon the use of 'precision strikes'.)

The closed fist covers more surface area than the open hand, creating more wind resistance as it ploughs through the air. Upon impact, the striking

Kempo-Jutsu.

energy is dispersed throughout the entire fist, rather than focused on a particular point. Many closed-fist striking techniques are taught in the elementary levels of Kempo-Jutsu. Ideally, if you were to use a closed fist to strike at an opponent, you would do so with the intention of hitting with the first two knuckles of the fist in order to achieve a more penetrating effect. Often, in practice, this fails to occur due to a lack of speed, accuracy and proximity to an opponent, and/or the quick movement of an opponent out of harm's way. The closed fist does, however, provide the 'student-level' practitioner a 'safe' way to strike because (1) the closed hand is

Impact area on fist.

less likely to be injured during a strike, and (2) its greater surface area makes it more likely to hit some part of its target.

In the context of real confrontation, Kempo-Jutsu provided a chance for a Samurai to begin to injure and distract his opponent, setting him up for follow-up techniques, which include the devastating throws, joint-locking and groundwork techniques of Aiki-Jujutsu.

Aiki-Jujutsu: Second Method of Defence

The next major step in the defensive strategy of the Samurai entailed sword disarming, referred to as 'Tachi Dori'. This technique involved seizing the Samurai sword from an opponent and using it against him or securing it from being drawn from its scabbard and subsequently performing an Aiki-Jujutsu throwing, joint-locking or choking technique. If an unarmed Samurai had been the opponent and there had been no sword to use in defence, the Aiki-Jujutsu technique would follow immediately subsequent to the Kempo-Jutsu evasive or invasive movement and strike.

I suggested earlier that the martial arts of Aiki-Jutsu and Ju-Jutsu manifest as the throwing and grappling elements of Aiki-Jujutsu, in which case one might wonder (1) what unique characteristics separate both martial arts into two distinct disciplines, and (2) can they really stand alone as two different martial arts? The following should provide some answers to these questions.

Tachi Dori.

Aiki-Jutsu throw.

Aiki-Jutsu

Aiki-Jutsu, the martial art of harmonizing or blending an opponent's energy with one's own internal energy, is used against an opponent who attacks with a perceivable momentum to a particular direction. Once the direction of the momentum or force is realized by the skilled Aiki-Ka, the Aiki practitioner, he blends with it and redirects it according to his needs, as opposed to colliding with the force, which would, in effect, 'stop it in its tracks'.

A practitioner of Aiki-Jutsu utilizes the striking and evasive techniques of Kempo-Jutsu in order to position his body close to an opponent. He then follows with linear, diagonal or circular movements to redirect an opponent's energy via a wrist or arm lock, throw or a combination of these techniques. There are two equally effective methods to facilitate an opponent's momentum from exhausting before redirecting the opponent or guiding the opponent along the same plane or path. One method is accomplished intuitively (having achieved 'Mushin' or 'no-mindedness' during uncontrived combat) by blending with an attack at the most opportune moment, when an opponent fully commits to a course of attack and cannot adjust to a different direction. The other method makes use of Atemi, the striking techniques of Kempo-Jutsu, to relax and distract an opponent just prior to an Aiki-Jutsu throw. An instantaneous, tactical choice of

strikes is employed to help shackle the opponent's momentum. The goal is to redirect or continue his movement in the same direction as he is already going, thereby committing the opponent *en route* into an Aiki-Jutsu technique. To the untrained eye, this method might create an illusion of stopping an opponent's momentum. In actuality, sometimes a technique requires one to slow an opponent's momentum in order to take control of his movement. As long as there is any degree of momentum, an opponent can be thrown masterfully into an Aiki-Jutsu technique.

Ju-Jutsu: Soft, Subtle, Economical

Ju-Jutsu (soft martial art) implies subtlety and the most economic use of force against an opponent. The meaning of Ju-Jutsu applies to the manner in which a skilled practitioner of the martial art manipulates an opponent's body by means of subtle, sometimes undetectable, nevertheless powerful movements. Ju-Jutsu-Ka, Jujutsu practitioners, are trained to detect subtle imbalances in an opponent's posture and to use this knowledge in order to further impose off-balancing techniques (Kuzushi). These techniques are employed with the objective of uprooting and throwing an opponent who might be trying to 'ground' himself. When I use the word 'ground' in this context, I am describing an opponent who might be situating himself into a deep, rooted stance and might not be applying an observable, forward momentum during his offensive. For example, a person who attacks in this way might be striking without advancing forward but rather via a twist of the hips. While this might not be a most powerful form of attack, it is a way in which an opponent might try to prevent his body from committing to any particular direction. This type of attack may have catalysed the development of Ju-Jutsu techniques.

The throwing techniques of Ju-Jutsu are almost completely dependent upon the Atemi of Kempo-Jutsu. In some cases, with masterful skill, the practitioner can apply Ju-Jutsu throwing techniques by blending with his opponent's energy, similar to the method described in Aiki-Jutsu. In most cases, applying an appropriate Ju-Jutsu throwing technique is contingent upon the direction in which the Atemi off-balanced the opponent. Subsequent to a strike, the opponent must be drawn into a smooth, jolt-free, non-stop throwing technique using Kuzushi and leveraging.

When one applies all of the elements that I have described to perform a throw, the opponent should feel light and yielding, provided that the opponent does not weigh more than one and a half times' the thrower's weight. In the case that an opponent's weight is at least twice the weight of the thrower, some Ju-Jutsu techniques can still be used effectively, provided that the correct choice of technique is applied. Ju-Jutsu can, therefore, be applied 'economically', enabling an individual of small stature to throw a person significantly larger than himself. Consider the following: if an individual were to attempt to lift something onto his shoulder that measured taller and weighed much more than himself, he might tilt it and lean it against his body in order to gain a firm grip. He could then bend his knees deeply, while attempting to keep the back of his body straight, in an attempt to prevent a strain to his lower back. The lifter could assume a wide stance for balance, tip the object onto his shoulder to the rear and balance it in a seesaw-like fashion. He might finally attempt to lift the object using the strength of his legs. The aforementioned is similar to the methodology that would be employed to lever an opponent over the back for a Ju-Jutsu throw.

Ju-Jutsu throw against a larger opponent.

CHAPTER 2

BUDO: MARTIAL WAYS

Having described the essence of Aiki-Jujutsu and the different classes of technique that comprise the breadth of the martial system, the next topic of discussion will be dedicated to how Budo (martial ways) expanded one step further, forming a sub-class or new generation of techniques and martial philosophy.

During the Meiji period, Bujutsu was stripped of its important role in the security of the Japanese nation, and Japan's values and priorities changed dramatically. The need for Bujutsu, the combat-effective martial arts technique developed to combat the sword-wielding Samurai, became obsolete and was replaced by more modern instruments of war.

The realization and acceptance of Japan's 'new vision' catalysed change in the manner in which the martial arts were practised and how they were applied to people's lives. As a consequence, Budo, evolving from its predecessor, Bujutsu, was born. Martial arts techniques were modified for aesthetic reasons and people began to contemplate the techniques, painstakingly studying each movement in order to learn why they worked and how the techniques might be improved upon. The efficacy of the techniques took on a less significant role, while much time was spent in contemplation of how they worked on energetic, physical and spiritual levels. The objective of martial arts training became oriented more toward the attainment of spiritual enlightenment and physical prowess than battle-readiness. The aspiration to 'perfect' techniques, by demonstrating them in a flawless and most economical fashion, became a goal as well.

While there are unique characteristics that differentiate Budo from Bujutsu, it is important to remember that a thorough study of Bujutsu contains all the characteristics of its (contemporary) Budo. The difference is a matter of perception and in the application of its techniques. In my study of Budo, I have observed that Budo tends to focus on a particular aspect of a Bujutsu predecessor, which I intend to elaborate upon as I describe the Budo that evolved from Aiki-Jutsu and Ju-Jutsu.

Aikido

Aikido (the way of harmonizing energy) naturally evolved from the techniques of Aiki-Jutsu, an aspect of the martial art of Aiki-Jujutsu. Its movements and throwing techniques were used to counter powerful, impending forces through the use of strong momentum, with the goal of redirecting an opponent. In the post-Meiji era, when martial arts practitioners were rarely in danger of being confronted by a swordsman, there was no need to practise defending against a sword-wielding attacker. There was, however, and still continues to be, a belief that the movements and varieties of defence techniques developed during real bouts had great value for the Budo-Ka (practitioner of Budo). Aikido, similar to other Budo, was developed with priorities differing from Bujutsu; however, certain aspects of Bujutsu were painstakingly preserved.

Most Aikido styles that are practised today emphasize the wrist-locking, arm-locking and throwing techniques that characterize the martial art of Aiki-Jutsu. In the case of an attempted strike to the head, however, Samurai sword-attack technique might be represented by the use of the edge of the hand (Shuto Uchi or knife-hand strike), simulating the motions of the sword. In other instances, a Bokken (a wooden Samurai sword replica) or Jo

Aikido throw (1).

Aikido throw (2).

(short staff) is used in a similar fashion. One of the primary objectives of Aikido training is to be able to learn how to react instantaneously to an attack and redirect or continue an opponent's energy into a throw or locking technique without striking the opponent. Conditioning the body to react naturally in response to overwhelming force, by using the principles of avoidance, yielding and the redirection of an attacker's momentum, are some of the fundamental precepts of the art form. The ability to relax and respond to multiple attacks with grace and fluidity is learned through 'Kata' (contrived practice) and then applied to Aiki-Randori (free-sparring), an uncontrived exercise that builds this skill. It is essential to remember that an opponent must be attacking with powerful momentum in order for the practitioner to perform an uninterrupted throw without striking his opponent.

Another aspect of Aikido practice focuses on Kansetsu Waza, the joint-locking techniques of Aiki-Jutsu. In this phase of training, most techniques are performed from a stationary position and attacks usually consist of grabs (as opposed to strikes) to different areas of the body. Different styles of Aikido

employ strikes, to varying degrees, as a retaliatory technique.

Aikido can naturally evolve from any style of Aiki-Jutsu and/or Aiki-Jujutsu and is practised outside the famous Ueshiba family tree. Similar to Judo, the subject of my next discussion, other styles are practised outside of the auspices of the Kodokan, the most famous style of Judo, developed by Jigoro Kano.

Judo: Gentle Way

Judo (gentle or soft way) evolved from the Aiki-Jujutsu techniques classified as Ju-Jutsu in the same way that Aikido proliferated from the Aiki-Jutsu component of Aiki-Jujutsu. The throwing techniques employed in Judo to uproot a more grounded opponent were practised and intellectualized in terms of how the practitioner might execute his technique in a most economical fashion, by generating enough Kuzushi (off-balancing) and leverage to throw an opponent.

Similar to Aikido, the earliest forms of Judo

Judo throw.

ments, teaching the practitioner to 'feel' where his opponent is moving without having to redirect his eyes toward that direction. This represents an important skill that is applicable while moving in for a throw to an opponent. In addition, Randori provides a vehicle through which to practise the application of Kuzushi and to leverage an opponent who is unwilling to fall unless he is compelled to do so involuntarily.

Some of the older styles of Judo still use striking techniques in their art, but this practical element has essentially been abandoned. Today Judo is practised mostly as a sport, with very little use of some of the more pragmatic characteristics of Ju-Jutsu.

More About Budo

Budo can be regarded as a way in which the contemporary Japanese of the time demonstrated their reverence and appreciation for the skill and techniques that were conceived of and developed by the Samurai, based upon their experiences in combat. It is a methodology that continues to take on new shapes, indirectly making use of the lessons of Bujutsu. Budo is multi-faceted; it is a way in which to enlighten the mind, exercise the body and soothe the soul. Budo may have begun as Bujutsu and first practised on the bare ground. From there, it may have moved on to the Tatame in a small Dojo (martial arts school), made its way to fame in the great Kodokan (Judo School in Japan) and then on to international Olympic status thereafter. It is important to keep in mind, however, that the majority of the original founders of Budo were aspiring to find enlightenment through the practice and lifestyle of the martial arts. Contemplation of the way in which techniques worked most efficiently, and then practising them to exhaustive lengths, became a meditative exercise, sometimes leading to an epiphany or a 'higher knowledge' of the martial arts. I have chosen, therefore, to characterize the martial arts as 'meditation in movement', with the practitioner exercising the body while simultaneously contemplating the movements.

Whether the martial artist is practising Randori

appeared almost identical to its predecessor martial art Ju-Jutsu with regard to strategy and technique but without the need for defensive techniques against the Samurai arsenal of weaponry. The objective of Judo focused on attaining physical, intellectual and spiritual enlightenment via training, which, similar to Aikido, gradually modified the way Ju-Jutsu techniques were practised. Dissimilar to Aikido, Judo's version of the Randori exercise evolved into a competitive sport between Judo-Ka (Judo players). Judo Randori commences with two Judo-Ka, each grabbing the other's uniform. This is accomplished through the use of one hand to grab the opponent's lapel and the other hand to grab the opponent's opposite sleeve. Each competitor tries to lure his opponent toward a particular direction in order to catch him off-balance. He then attempts to guide him into a throw, finishing with a submission hold on the Tatame (mats).

Outside the context of competition, the practice of Judo Randori can be an important tool for the student of Judo and Ju-Jutsu. The exercise enhances the body's sensitivity to another person's move-with a partner or training solo, he is connecting with the energy that surrounds him, with the Spirit with which we all connect and feel at home… he is connecting with The Infinite.

It is my opinion that every element of Budo that I have described is as much a part of Bujutsu as it is Budo. While these elements are the hallmarks of Budo, they are only a few of the 'building blocks' that comprise the thickly woven fabric of Bujutsu.

While I haven't lived the life of a Samurai, I believe that each Samurai had a different load of duties, providing for more or less time for contemplation, meditation and the consequent development of the hallmarks of Budo.

It is my contention that Bujutsu is the most complete manifestation of the Japanese martial arts and the Ryu the most profound conglomeration of these martial arts into a comprehensive system.

Meditation.

PART II

KEMPO-JUTSU

Now that you have a better understanding of how the individual arts classified as Budo naturally evolved from Bujutsu, let us look carefully at Fukasa-Ryu Kempo-Jutsu in order to understand its place in the system of Fukasa-Ryu Aiki-Jujutsu.

CHAPTER 3

FUKASA-RYU KEMPO-JUTSU

I have explained that Kempo-Jutsu is a combination of tactical, evasive and invasive movements that are performed in tandem with blocks and strikes; the latter position the body for a throwing, joint-locking or sword-disarming technique. The strategy of Fukasa-Ryu Kempo-Jutsu is to evade an impending attack by moving out of the way to a position close enough to deliver a powerful striking technique, Atemi (strike), in response. The evasive movement should employ a minimum number of steps or shifts, moving from posture to posture, exemplifying correct Kempo-Jutsu form. This will ensure a swift and economical movement, resulting in a grounded stance, perfect for an effective striking technique. The practitioner should now be positioned for a throwing, joint-locking or sword-disarming technique to follow.

This sequence of blocking while moving invasively, striking and then throwing and so on, is an effective protocol to be employed by students of any style of Aiki-Jujutsu in order to successfully ward off an attack. There are, however, circumstances that might not follow this model, in which case a strike might not be needed before performing a throw; for example: (1) if the practitioner is able to perform the technique at the precise, opportune moment when an attacker might be committing to a move using powerful momentum, or (2) if the practitioner moves out of the way to evade an attack and simultaneously invades with the goal of striking his opponent, eliminating a need for a blocking technique, or (3) on an occasion when a block might be followed by a few strikes, which might render an opponent 'down for the count' with no need for any follow-up techniques.

Each one of these scenarios is a possibility, and the mind of the Fukasa-Ryu Aiki-Jujutsu-Ka must be conditioned to be resolute and thorough in response to an attack. Every element of the practitioner's arsenal of knowledge must be quickly accessed in order to efficiently and effectively extinguish an impending threat.

Blocking Strategy

The method of blocking espoused by Fukasa-Ryu originated with C.R. Marshall, Shihan, a mentor from my earliest years as a martial artist: 'The practitioner must not fight fire with fire, which only makes it more ablaze. He must fight fire with water.' While combating energy with a quantitatively larger measure of energy might, in some cases, be a successful strategy of defence, meeting force with overwhelming force potentially results in greater chaos, injury to persons involved and the possibility of 'collateral damage' as an unnecessary consequence.

A system of Aiki-Jujutsu must enable an individual of any stature to defend against an opponent of any size. The Asian martial arts are famous for empowering and leading to victory against the largest of men, individuals who might, at first glance, be superficially perceived by their opponents as underdogs. The primary objective of Fukasa-Ryu Kempo-Jutsu is to move the practitioner's body out of the way of an opponent's fury of strikes to close proximity, within striking range of the opponent. This manoeuvre allows for a strong, penetrating strike and easy grab to the opponent's limbs or clothing as preparation for a throw or joint-locking technique. The objective is to get as close as possible to the opponent, within grabbing distance, so that it is difficult for an attacker to direct dangerous blows to the body of his potential victim. Proximity to the attacker would

Hidari Hanmi Dachi (against an opponent).

render an attack unlikely due to the lack of space needed to chamber the legs and cock the arms for a powerful strike.

The untrained martial artist might perceive this invasive tactic to be perilous, arguing that it might put the body at risk of being within 'arms reach' of the attacker. It is a fact that many athletes in martial sports tend to use their legs in competition in order to keep their attackers 'at bay'. This is done to prevent the opponent from closing in and penetrating the 'aura' or invisible energy field surrounding the body. While it is important to recognize and accept the fact that too much distance between practitioner and opponent does not allow for damaging strikes to the opponent's body, the practitioner must come within an attacker's reach in order to deliver a devastating blow. The martial artist must, therefore, be resolute as well as a positive thinker, and react without hesitation and fear in order to effectively defend against an attacker, irrespective of his stature.

Posture and State of Mind

The manner in which the body is situated into a stance prior to an attack, while performing martial arts techniques and after a force has been extinguished, will have great bearing upon whether or not the practitioner can safely protect himself in a successful and economical fashion. Of equal importance is the state of the practitioner's mind, which should be relaxed yet prepared to react spontaneously with little cognitive effort; there is no room for hesitation, and complete confidence is critical to maintaining one's defence.

An ideal state of readiness is exemplified by the meaning of Mushin (no-mindedness), a state of just 'being', present, ready and confident in one's self. This implies having no expectations of any particular type of attack, being resolute, prepared to overcome anything with which one may be confronted. The Fukasa-Ryu style has a fitting stance, enabling its practitioners to just 'be' in this relaxed, yet alert, state of readiness. From Shizentai Dachi, a natural, 'at ease' posture, with arms hanging relaxed at the sides and legs spread about the width of the shoulders, the practitioner can easily poise himself, ready for an attack if a confrontation should escalate to a need for a physical response. The 'hands relaxed' position facilitates relaxation of the mind and body, and the location of the hands at the hips facilitates a commitment-free stance. Dissimilar to fighting stances that require perching the hands high in front of the chest, serving to protect the upper region of the body, Hidari Hanmi Dachi is assumed with the hands relaxed at the sides, and the feet narrowly placed and aligned at the heels. This versatile posture enables the practitioner to quickly move in any direction in tandem with a block and strike.

Alternatively, the 'Western boxer stance,' with the hands mounted up at the front of the body, keeps the weapons (the hands) visible to the opponent as opposed to being at the more stealthy position (Kempo-Jutsu posture), below eye level, at the side of the body. The advantage of this Kempo-Jutsu posture is that the crude, more primitive attacker, perceiving the hands to be hanging lazily at the sides, might interpret the posture as a lack of readiness, compelling him to foolishly 'over commit', with his defences down. This would provide an easily resolved scenario for the Kempo-Jutsu-ka, Kempo-Jutsu practitioner. Against a sword or knife attack, the Kempo-Jutsu-Ka would prefer a full thrust or swing of the Samurai sword as opposed to a slash by a swordsman or a knife-wielding opponent, who is trying to keep his distance by using his weapon.

The goal of the Kempo-Jutsu-Ka is to lure his opponent into a full-fledged attack, committing the opponent's body into a forward movement. Situating the arms at the sides of the body and keeping the legs in a narrow stance protects the limbs from the danger of being slashed from a distance. This position forces an attacker to come closer, giving the Kempo-Jutsu-Ka the proximity to retaliate powerfully. The practitioner of the Fukasa-Ryu system is taught to assume a fighting posture by directing his chest slightly toward the right, with the left foot forward. In this position, as a first mode of defence, the heart, now shifted out of harm's way, can be protected. The Samurai viewed the heart as an important life-sustaining organ, which is why the Samurai sword was affixed to the left side of the Samurai's body to protect the heart.

Earlier, I briefly alluded to the possibility of a confrontation being resolved before it escalates to a physical level. In contemporary life, the likelihood of being attacked by a Samurai sword would appear to be quite remote. Baseball bats and knives, however, which are sometimes used as instruments of violence, can be defended against with techniques similar to those that were once used against the Samurai sword. From a legal standpoint, an individual observed to have a non-aggressive posture prior to a physical altercation would probably have a better chance at winning the confidence of a jury. I contend that the Bu-Jutsu-Ka martial artist, with adequate skill and peace of mind, should be able to extinguish an attack before it elevates to a physical level.

As I think retrospectively about the confrontations that have come my way in day-to-day life, I feel that the relaxed and confident posture that I have been describing has, for me, portrayed a confidence and resoluteness that was often instrumental in thwarting confrontation before it elevated to a physical level. Through my own personal experience, I have observed that a calm demeanour and the appearance of readiness in the face of confrontation have created anxiety and a loss of confidence in my potential opponents. I sense that my less than average weight of 123lb (55kg) and height of 5ft 6in (182cm) do not typically represent a person of strength to those who pass me by during my day-to-day travels. Those who have misjudged me by virtue of my small stature, however, have apparently been sufficiently impressed by my resoluteness and calmness under the pressure of confrontation that they have chosen to desist in escalating provocative behaviour. Permit my personal experience to provide validation for my contention that 'stance' is pivotal to the success of the Kempo-Jutsu-Ka.

Dachi Waza: Stances

Shizentai Dachi: Natural Stance

Shizentai Dachi is assumed by standing relaxed with the legs slightly bent (approximating the width of the shoulders) and the arms hanging relaxed at the sides. This posture is the starting point from which we reposition into the postures that follow.

Shizentai Dachi.

Hidari Hanmi Dachi.   *Migi Hanmi Dachi.*

right foot back to a rear, right, oblique direction. The right knee is straightened or 'locked' and the right foot is pointed to the front, right, oblique direction, at a 45-degree angle relative to the front of the body. The left foot is pointed straight ahead, beyond the front of the body, and the left knee is bent deeply. The width of the posture is such that the practitioner can hold his balance from a light push to the sides of his body. Migi Zenkutsu Dachi (right forward stance) is assumed in a fashion similar to that described for the left side, but with the right foot forward.

Hidari Hanmi Dachi: Left Half-Body Stance

Hidari Hanmi Dachi is an ideal posture, when poised for a first mode of defence, because it allows the practitioner to shift the heart out of harm's way. To assume this position from Shizentai Dachi, be sure that your left foot is pointed straight ahead and beyond the front of the body. Shift the right foot approximately 3 or 4in (8–10cm) behind the left foot and turn it to a 45-degree angle relative to the front of the body. The heels of both feet are vertically aligned and the knees are comfortably bent, with slightly more weight resting on the back leg. The arms hang naturally at the sides of the body with the hands open and the palms facing the body at the side of the legs. Migi Hanmi Dachi (right half-body stance) is assumed in a fashion similar to that described for the left side, but with the right foot forward.

Zenkutsu Dachi: Forward 'Locked-Leg' Stance

Zenkutsu Dachi is a grounded posture that is stabilized by the back foot resting flat on its sole, with the back knee extended straight. It is utilized to generate power in a forward direction… power that can be used for striking and throwing purposes. The practitioner assumes Hidari Zenkutsu Dachi (left forward stance) from Shizentai Dachi by sliding the

Hidari Zenkutsu Dachi.

Migi Zenkutsu Dachi.

LEFT: Hidari Jigotai Dachi.

RIGHT: Migi Jigotai Dachi.

Jigotai Dachi: Defensive 'Square' Stance

Jigotai Dachi is a wide stance, with the heels of the feet positioned equidistant to the body's centre, and the body weight resting evenly on each leg. To assume Hidari Jigotai Dachi (left defensive stance) from Shizentai Dachi, straighten the left foot so that it points forward. Slide the right foot far back to the right, rear, oblique direction and twist it so that the foot points to the right. The practitioner bends the knees of both legs in such a way that the kneecaps would obscure the toes if he were to peer down at them. Migi Jigotai Dachi (right defensive stance) is assumed in a fashion similar to that described for the left side, but with the right foot forward.

Kosa Dachi: Cross Stance

From Shizentai, Hidari Kosa Dachi (left cross stance) is assumed by twisting the left foot so that it points to the front, left, oblique direction. Slide the right foot behind the left foot and position it slightly toward the left direction, so the front of the right knee fits snugly against the back of the left knee. The right foot rests on its ball, with its heel positioned off the Tatame (mat) and both knees bent deeply for stability. Migi Kosa Dachi (right cross stance) is assumed in a fashion similar to that described for the left side, but with the right foot forward.

Hidari Kosa Dachi.

Migi Kosa Dachi.

Jigohontai Dachi.

Jigohontai Dachi: Neutral Stance

Jigohontai Dachi is a stance used to 'root' the body in order to maintain balance during certain throwing techniques. It enables the practitioner to generate power for a throw and makes it difficult for an opponent to pull the practitioner down. From Shizentai Dachi, spread the legs to a comfortable width and

Migi Kokutsu Dachi.

position the feet so that they face forward. Keeping the back straight, bend the knees so that the toes are obscured from view by the kneecaps.

Kokutsu Dachi: Back Stance

From Shizentai Dachi, assume Hidari Kokutsu Dachi (left back stance) by sliding the right foot back into Hidari Jigotai Dachi. Turn the left (front) foot and direct it toward the right, oblique direction. Straighten the left leg and bend the right knee deeply. Migi Kokutsu Dachi (right back stance) is performed in a similar fashion, but with the right foot forward.

Hidari Kokutsu Dachi.

Atemi Waza: Hand Striking Techniques

Seiken: Fist

The closed fist in Fukasa-Ryu is held with the pinky, ring and middle fingers folded tightly into the palm of the hand. The index finger is bent at the first and second knuckles, but the knuckle that is located closest to the fingertip is kept straightened, with the fingertip resting on the palm of the hand. The thumb is bent and lies across the topside of the index finger, tightly sandwiching the index finger between itself and the middle finger. This method

Seiken.

Fist clinch 1.

Fist clench 2.

Fist completely closed.

of clenching the fist stabilizes the large knuckles of the index and middle fingers for striking impact. It evolved from Okinawan Karate, with the objective of preventing the knuckles from sustaining damage as they impact with their target. The fist is tightened in this fashion in Fukasa-Ryu Kempo-Jutsu for this very reason. Dissimilar to many forms of Karate, in which the fist is twisted into a horizontal orientation just subsequent to impact with a target, Fukasa-Ryu Kempo-Jutsu uses the fist, almost exclusively, in a vertical orientation.

The following striking techniques will be demonstrated from Hidari Hanmi Dachi, the ideal, combat-ready stance.

Migi Oi Tate Tsuki: Right Vertical Lunging Fist Strike

From Hidari Hanmi Dachi, slide the right foot on its ball to the front, right, oblique direction, situating into Migi Zenkutsu Dachi. At the same time, elevate the left open hand, position it to the front of the left side of the head, and close and extend the right fist to strike.

Depending upon the proximity of the body relative to an opponent, it might be necessary to slide the back foot slightly forward to the right, oblique direction to avoid over-extending the stance and bending your back to reach an opponent. This will also position the body out of 'harm's way' if

Migi Joden Oi Tate Tsuki.

Migi Chuden Oi Tate Tsuki.

Migi Gedan Oi Tate Tsuki.

the opponent should attempt a linear attack using multiple strikes. Be mindful not to cock the right hand around the area of the ribcage. It should thrust forward from the proximity of the hips in a smooth, fluid motion, and the fist should gradually close in preparation for impact. This increases striking speed because an already tightened fist creates a stiff arm that slows the momentum of a strike significantly.

The left, open hand is positioned to the front of the left side of the head because the majority of opponents that might be encountered outside of the Dojo (martial arts school) are not trained fighters. They would tend to use the roundhouse variety of strikes, as opposed to straight punches. The defensive hand is positioned as described in anticipation of the most likely mode of attack.

Migi Oi Tate Tsuki can be easily adjusted to hit targets to the upper, middle and lower quadrants of an opponent's body. For Migi Joden Oi Tate Tsuki (right upper-level vertical lunging fist strike), direct the strike upward toward the opponent's face or neck area. For Migi Chuden Oi Tate Tsuki (right middle-level vertical lunging fist strike), the fist should elevate only to the level of the sternum. For Migi Gedan Oi Tate Tsuki (right lower-level vertical lunging fist strike), the fist should impact an opponent at approximately the level of the 'hara' (lower abdominal cavity) or the upper region of the legs.

For each type of strike, an attempt should be made to hit the opponent using the first two knuckles only, thereby decreasing the surface area of the strike and centralizing all the power into this small area. This technique yields a precise strike with a penetrating effect to the opponent's body. Steering

the knuckles toward a target requires a slight, inward bend of the wrist, directing the knuckles forward. A bent wrist also protects the wrist from injury when the fist impacts the target; a straightened wrist risks injury. In order to prevent hyper-extension of the forearm and elbow when a strike of this variety is being performed, the arm extends only to the point at which the elbow is still slightly bent. A 'locked elbow' can easily be broken by an opponent, and the practitioner with a 'locked elbow' risks tearing the connective tissue in his own forearm, should he miss his target.

Hidari Oi Tate Tsuki: Left Vertical Lunging Fist Strike

The same variety of strikes is employed similarly using the left fist. Striking with the left fist requires that the right, open hand be positioned to the front of the right side of the head, while closing and extending the left fist to strike. At the same time, the left foot slides to the front, left, oblique direction to assume Hidari Zenkutsu Dachi.

Note: in Fukasa-Ryu Kempo-Jutsu, all strikes are performed from Hidari Hamni Dachi regardless of which hand the practitioner is using to perform a strike. For the left fist, to employ Joden (upper-level), Chuden (middle-level) and Gedan (lower-level) Oi Tate Tsuki, the fist would be directed to each quadrant of the opponent's body in a fashion similar to the way it was described using the right fist.

Gyaku Tsuki: Reverse Strikes

In Fukasa-Ryu Kempo-Jutsu, reverse strikes are

Hidari Joden Oi Tate Tsuki.

Hidari Chuden Oi Tate Tsuki.

Hidari Gedan Oi Tate Tsuki.

employed through the generation of power that originates from the twisting motion of the hips. These strikes are used when an opponent is situated too close to the practitioner's body and there is no space in which to slide forward in order to execute a strike. The strikes are most frequently used as 'follow-up' strikes or as a combination of multiple strikes, and they are accomplished by twisting the body in place on the balls of the feet, allowing for quick and explosive strikes. The right and left hands are employed in sequence.

It is important to mention that Fukasa-Ryu Kempo-Jutsu advocates the use of reverse strikes far less frequently than lunging strikes that use the body's forward momentum. The strike using the forward momentum of the body allows for the most efficient use of the practitioner's body weight. Used as a first strike to an opponent, the lunging strike tactically positions the practitioner's body close enough to grab the opponent.

Hidari Gyaku Tate Tsuki: Left Reverse Vertical Fist Strike

From Hidari Hanmi Dachi, the right foot slides out to the right, oblique direction to assume Migi Zenkutsu Dachi. Once in this posture, the right, open hand elevates to the front of the right side of the head, as the hips twist clockwise on the ball of the left foot in order to strike the opponent using the left fist. As the hips twist for the strike, the stance deepens, and the left elbow does not extend too far forward beyond the front of the body. As the arm extends farther from the body, the power of the strike gradually decreases. This occurs because the power is then derived from the triceps alone rather than the whole of the body's weight.

Hidari Joden Gyaku Tate Tsuki (left upper-level reverse vertical fist strike), Hidari Chuden Gyaku Tate Tsuki (left middle-level reverse vertical fist strike) and Hidari Gedan Gyaku Tate Tsuki (left lower-level reverse vertical fist strike) are all performed using this method.

Hidari Joden Gyaku Tate Tsuki.

Hidari Chuden Gyaku Tate Tsuki.

Hidari Gedan Gyaku Tate Tsuki.

Migi Joden Gyaku Tate Tsuki.

Migi Chuden Gyaku Tate Tsuki.

Migi Gedan Gyaku Tate Tsuki.

Hidari Joden Oi Kage Tsuki.

Migi Joden Oi Kage Tsuki.

Hidari Gedan Oi Kage Tsuki.

Migi Gyaku Tate Tsuki: Right Reverse Vertical Fist Strike

From Hidari Hanmi Dachi, slide the left foot forward to the front, left, oblique direction to assume Hidari Zenkutsu Dachi. Raise the left hand to the front of the left side of the head and twist the hips counterclockwise to strike using the right fist. Bend the right knee and twist deeply on the balls of the foot for stability and power as the strike is directed to the upper, middle or lower quadrants of the opponent's body (Migi Joden Gyaku Tate Tsuki, Migi Chuden Gyaku Tate Tsuki or Migi Gedan Gyaku Tate Tsuki).

Oi Kage Tsuki: Lunging Hook Strike

Migi and Hidari Oi Kage Tsuki are performed by 'hooking' the fist around from the side of the body in order to target the upper and lower regions of an opponent's body: Hidari Joden Oi Kage Tsuki (left upper-level lunging hook strike), Migi Joden

Migi Gedan Oi Kage Tsuki.

Oi Kage Tsuki (right upper-level lunging hook strike), Hidari Gedan Oi Kage Tsuki (left lower-level lunging hook strike) and Migi Gedan Oi Kage Tsuki (right lower-level lunging hook strike). Similar to a 'roundhouse' type of punch, it circles toward its target from the sides of the body, as opposed to travelling on a straight, linear plane. Oi Kage Tsuki, however, utilizes a tighter circle and is more controlled than a wild roundhouse punch. The latter is a technique that might cock back and crank around, travelling in a wide, circular motion toward its target.

The footwork used to perform this strike is identical to the method that I described for use with the straight, lunging strikes in this section. The 'defensive hand' is likewise positioned at the front of the side of the head.

Gyaku Kage Tsuki: Reverse Hook Strike

Gyaku Kage Tsuki is performed using the same footwork as Gyaku Tate Tsuki and the same handwork as Oi Kage Tsuki – see illustrations of Migi Joden Gyaku Kage Tsuki (right upper-level reverse hook strike), Migi Gedan Gyaku Kage Tsuki (right lower-level reverse hook strike), Hidari Joden Gyaku Kage Tsuki (left upper-level reverse hook strike) and Hidari Gedan Gyaku Kage Tsuki (left lower-level reverse hook strike).

Migi Joden Gyaku Kage Tsuki.

Migi Gedan Gyaku Kage Tsuki.

Hidari Joden Gyaku Kage Tsuki.

Hidari Gedan Gyaku Kage Tsuki.

Geri Waza: Kicking Techniques

In Fukasa-Ryu Kempo-Jutsu, kicking techniques and strikes using the knees are secondary to striking techniques that use the hands and arms. The momentary lifting of the feet from the ground that characterizes strikes with the legs, creates a potential for instability that renders these strikes less preferable.

Fukasa-Ryu advocates the use of kicks only (1) when an opponent is out of reach of the hands, or (2) if the hands are preoccupied. As a rule of thumb, kicks should be directed only at the opponent's groin or legs; the higher the practitioner directs his kicks at an opponent, the more he risks being struck to the groin and leg or being thrown completely off-balance by the opponent. A kick to an area above the opponent's groin could be advantageous, however, if the opponent were doubled over on his knees or lying on the ground, distracted by an injury.

Kicks can be effective at warding-off grabs and chokes to the front, sides and back of the body. They can also be used as stealthy techniques, since they occur below an opponent's line of vision, thus catching the opponent off-guard.

A quick word to the wise: if a challenge arises, and you get into an altercation that cannot be resolved by anything but a physical response, keep in mind that we would have been created with wings if we were meant to fly. Stand on two feet, and do not ever use kicking techniques that involve flying, jumps or drops to the ground; you will just be making yourself more vulnerable to injury.

Mae Kekomi Geri: Front Thrust Kick

Migi Mae Kekomi Geri (right front thrust kick) is performed from Hidari Hanmi Dachi by turning the left foot slightly to the left, oblique direction, which prepares the body for a straight and stable kick directed to the opponent's groin or legs. The right knee is elevated, so the quadriceps of the leg are parallel to the ground. The right foot then thrusts forward by straightening the leg at the knee and ankles. The toes of the right foot are bent back, so the impact to the opponent's body is delivered with the ball of the foot as opposed to easily broken toes. Recover from the thrust by bringing the right foot back to touch the left leg lightly, momentarily assuming Tsuru Uke (crane block position) with the right knee positioned high in order to protect the groin from an unexpected strike from an opponent. Complete the technique by dropping the right foot forward to assume Migi Hanmi Dachi and draw the back, left leg slightly forward in order to cease the momentum of the technique and settle into the stance. This kick is typically performed with the hands protecting the front of the body, held around the level of the hara. The hands return to the sides of the body after recovering into Migi Hanmi Dachi.

Migi Mae Kekomi Geri (foot turn).

Migi Mae Kekomi Geri (lift leg).

Migi Mae Kekomi Geri (thrust).

Migi Mae Kekomi Geri (crane position).

Migi Mae Kekomi Geri (finish).

Hidari Mae Kekomi Geri

Mae Kekomi Geri can be performed using the left foot without having to adjust the posture; Hidari Hanmi Dachi, however, is done in a slightly different manner. Slide the right foot forward behind the left foot, creating a forward momentum, so that the left foot can rise and thrust forward toward its target. Be sure to lift your hands to protect the front of the body just as the right foot begins its motion. In this case, the left hand is positioned in front of the right hand because its position relative to the right hand is congruent to the leg that is doing the kicking. Recover by lightly tapping the right shin in order to safely transition from the kick forward into Hidari Hanmi Dachi. Once again, be sure to draw the back leg slightly forward in order to reassume Hidari Hanmi Dachi and slow the momentum of the body.

Hidari Mae Kekomi Geri (slide behind).

Hidari Mae Kekomi Geri (lift leg).

Hidari Mae Kekomi Geri (thrust).

Hidari Mae Kekomi Geri (recover).

Hidari Hanmi Dachi.

Mawashi Geri: Roundhouse Kick

From Hidari Hanmi Dachi, Migi Mawashi Geri (right roundhouse kick) is performed by turning the left foot in the left direction in order to prepare for a counterclockwise twist of the hips. The right knee is raised as the back of the body tilts approximately 45 degrees to the rear. As the body twists counterclockwise, it is balanced by the left leg. The right knee straightens and the foot extends forward, with toes bent back preparing for impact with the ball of the foot. The technique concludes by retracting the right foot and straightening the body upright into the crane block position (in order to protect the groin and genitalia). Migi Hanmi Dachi is assumed by lowering the right leg to the front of the body and drawing the left leg forward to bring the body to a halt. Slide the right foot to the rear direction to reassume Hidari Hanmi Dachi.

Hidari Mawashi Geri (left roundhouse kick) can also be performed from Hidari Hanmi Dachi. However, in order to duplicate the 'roundhouse' kicking motion described using the right foot, the left kick requires that the practitioner 'tiger step'. This is accomplished by using the right foot to slide forward and beyond the left foot into a tight posture, crossing both legs, with the left knee bent deeply to touch the upper part of the right calf. The power for the kick is generated by a rapid clockwise twist of the hips, unwinding the legs for a strong roundhouse kick using the left foot. Recover by transitioning into the left crane block position and then lower the left leg to the front of the body into Hidari Hanmi Dachi. Draw the right leg slightly forward to stop the body's momentum.

Regardless of which foot the practitioner is using to perform a kick, the leg that supports the kick is bent deeply enough to prevent the groin and supporting leg from becoming vulnerable to an attack as the

Migi Mawashi Geri (foot turn).

Migi Mawashi Geri (twist and lift leg).

Migi Mawashi Geri (thrust).

Migi Mawashi Geri (crane position).

Migi Hanmi Dachi (finish).

Hidari Mawashi Geri (tiger step).

Hidari Mawashi Geri (twist and lift leg).

Hidari Mawashi Geri (thrust).

kicking leg is extended toward its target. Note that there is a converse relationship between the height of a kick and the degree to which the supporting leg and groin become vulnerable to an attack. Be sure, therefore, to keep the knees bent and do not kick higher than required!

Similar to Mae Kekomi Geri, Mawashi Geri is meant to strike at areas below an opponent's waist, at the groin and legs. Only the ball of the foot is used to strike an opponent with these kicks. Do not curl the toes down and try to use the top of the foot in order to strike an opponent. This is a weak area of the foot and may lead to injury. The shin can, however, be used to strike the opponent if the practitioner finds himself relatively close to his target.

Kansetsu Geri: Joint Kick

Kansetsu Geri is most often used to break the main joint of the legs, i.e. the knees. In order to do so, the kick is directed to the front and sides of the knees and to the shins. This kick needs to be extra powerful due to the strength of the human leg. 'Locking', straightening the leg at the knee, maximizes the thrusting power of the kick. In every circumstance, the heel of the foot is used to deliver the devastating blow.

Migi Kansetsu Geri (right joint kick) is performed from Hidari Hanmi Dachi by positioning the left, front foot to the left, oblique direction. Lift the right knee high, aligning the thigh parallel to the ground, and bend the toes upward, directing the heel downward. Thrust the foot forward in a downward, diagonal direction, twisting the right leg counterclockwise as it extends toward its target. Strike the opponent using the heel of the foot and be sure the toes are curled upward on impact.

Migi Kansetsu Geri (foot turn).

Migi Kansetsu Geri (twist and lift leg).

Migi Kansetsu Geri (thrust).

Migi Kansetsu Geri (crane position).

Migi Hanmi Dachi (finish).

Retract the leg upward into the crane block position and follow by lowering the leg down to the front of the body to assume Migi Hanmi Dachi.

Reassume Hidari Hanmi Dachi by sliding the right foot in the rear direction.

Hidari Kansetsu Geri (left joint kick) is typically used as a follow-up strike if the practitioner is positioned in Migi Hanmi Dachi subsequent to a technique. Because great strength is needed to injure an opponent's leg, this kick is performed using only the leg that is positioned at the rear of the body. From Migi Hanmi Dachi, Hidari Kansetsu Geri is performed in a manner similar to that described for using the right foot.

Migi Hanmi Dachi.

Hidari Kansetsu Geri (twist and lift leg).

Hidari Kansetsu Geri (thrust).

Hidari Kansetsu Geri (crane position).

Hidari Hanmi Dachi (finish).

Yoko Kekomi Geri: Side Thrust Kick

Migi Yoko Kekomi Geri (right side thrust kick) is performed in a manner similar to Migi Kansetsu Geri. It is, however, directed straight out, horizontally, from the front of the body and positioned parallel to the Tatame, as opposed to downward toward its target. This kick is sometimes aimed at the upper part of the sides of the legs, but its main function in Fukasa-Ryu Kempo-Jutsu is as a secondary, 'follow-up' strike to the ribcage or head after an opponent keels over or falls to his knees.

From Hidari Hanmi Dachi, Hidari Yoko Kekomi Geri (left side thrust kick) is performed by sliding with the ball of the right foot behind and to the left

Hidari Hanmi Dachi.

Migi Yoko Kekomi Geri (twist foot).

Migi Yoko Kekomi Geri (twist and lift leg).

Migi Yoko Kekomi Geri (thrust).

Migi Yoko Kekomi Geri (crane position).

Migi Hanmi Dachi (finish).

Hidari Yoko Kekomi Geri (cross legs).

Hidari Yoko Kekomi Geri (lift leg).

Hidari Yoko Kekomi Geri (crane position).

of the left foot, similar to Kosa Dachi (cross stance). The right foot is positioned flat on its sole and the left foot is raised to the crane block position, with the left kneecap pointed to the right. With the left leg positioned sideways, the left kick is directed to the original direction beyond the front of the body. The right leg is bent to a height corresponding to the target, yet deeply enough for balance, so the practitioner's groin is not vulnerable to an attack. After the left leg is fully extended, 'locked' for power, the leg is drawn back into the crane block posture, with the left kneecap directed toward the right. Reassume Hidari Hanmi Dachi by turning toward the original, front direction, and lowering the left foot into position on to the Tatame. Drag the right foot slightly forward to slow the forward momentum of the technique.

Hidari Yoko Kekomi Geri (thrust).

Hidari Hanmi Dachi (finish).

Ushiro Kekomi Geri: Rear Thrust Kick

Ushiro Kekomi Geri (rear thrust kick) is most often used to counter rear chokes and grabs, as well as other 'surprise' attacks to the back of the body that require a quick, uninhibited response. Because there is virtually no way to prepare for a surprise attack from the rear, Ushiro Kekomi Geri is practised from Shizentai Dachi, a relatively relaxed posture. From Shizentai Dachi, the practitioner has time to more

easily transition into a posture such as Hidari Hanmi Dachi and use this kick. From Shizentai Dachi, lift either leg to the crane block position, directing the knee to front of the body. Curl the toes upward, directing the heel in a downward direction. Look over the shoulder that corresponds to the leg that is being used for the kick and, while tilting the body so that the head is directed forward, thrust the heel straight back to its target, straightening the leg at

Shizentai Dachi.

Migi Ushiro Kekomi Geri (lift leg).

Migi Ushiro Kekomi Geri (thrust).

Migi Ushiro Kekomi Geri (crane position).

Migi Hanmi Dachi (finish).

Hidari Ushiro Kekomi Geri (lift leg).

Hidari Ushiro Kekomi Geri (thrust).

Hidari Ushiro Kekomi Geri (crane position).

Hidari Hanmi Dachi (finish).

43

the knee. Similar to Yoko Kekomi Geri, the kicking leg is held parallel to the ground as it impacts with its target. In addition, the height of the kick can be adjusted by bending the knee of the 'supporting leg'. This kick is usually directed at an opponent's groin, but it can be used to strike the ribs and face, if the practitioner lowers his body by falling to the knees or dropping to the ground. Upon impacting the opponent, the foot is pointed downward and the ankles are bent so that the heel points to the rear direction. Recover by retracting the foot back toward the body and uprighting the body to either the right or left crane block position, depending upon which leg was used to perform the kick. If the right foot has been used to perform the kick, twist the body clockwise to face the original, rear direction, drop the right foot forward into Migi Hanmi Dachi and draw the left foot slightly forward in order to stop the momentum of the technique. A counterclockwise twist of the body to reassume

Hidari Hanmi Dachi to the original rear direction would be required if the left foot had been used to perform the kick.

The kick can also be performed from Hidari Hanmi Dachi. For Migi Ushiro Kekomi Geri (right rear thrust kick), slide the left foot straight back, lightly on its ball, so that the foot is situated close to the right foot. Situate the left foot flat on its sole and lift the right leg, positioning the body into the crane block posture, with the right knee pointing forward, beyond the front of the body. Perform the kick using the right foot in a manner similar to that described for Shizentai Dachi. Recover into the crane block position and twist clockwise to reassume Migi Hanmi Dachi to the original, rear direction.

To perform Hidari Ushiro Kekomi Geri (left rear thrust kick) from Hidari Hanmi Dachi, bend the right knee and lift the left leg into the crane block position. Extend the left foot to the rear direction in exactly the same manner as described using the

Hidari Hanmi Dachi.

Migi Ushiro Kekomi Geri (lift leg).

Migi Ushiro Kekomi Geri (thrust).

Migi Ushiro Kekomi Geri (crane postion).

Migi Hanmi Dachi (finish).

Hidari Hanmi Dachi.

Hidari Ushiro Kekomi Geri (lift leg).

Hidari Ushiro Kekomi Geri (thrust).

right foot. Recover by straightening the body and bringing the left knee back to the crane block position. Twist the body counterclockwise and resituate into Hidari Hanmi Dachi, slowing the momentum by drawing the right leg forward into position.

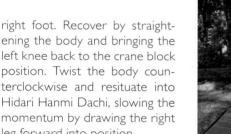

Hidari Ushiro Kekomi Geri (crane position).

Hidari Hanmi Dachi (finish).

Striking Strategy

At this point, it would be appropriate to consider how the practitioner's choice of strikes, used to retaliate against an opponent's attack, might affect the next retaliatory measure he might take to ward-off an attacker. When I discussed earlier the general strategy of Fukasa-Ryu Kempo-Jutsu, I suggested that striking is used to set up an opponent for an Aiki-Jujutsu throw. When a practitioner chooses a strike, he should know how it should affect his opponent, assuming the strike was on target and powerful enough of a blow.

It has been my experience that strong, linear strikes, impacting to an opponent's ribs, cause an opponent to fall over in a forward direction, while linear strikes, to an opponent's face and throat, generally result in an opponent stumbling back to his rear. Strikes that hook from the sides of the body and impact to the sides of the opponent's head or chin result in an opponent stumbling to an oblique, rear direction or to the sides. Strong, hooking strikes, that impact to the sides of the ribcage, cause an opponent to keel over to the side to which the strike had been directed. Kicks to the groin cause opponents to fall over and forward, and strong kicks to the legs can force an opponent onto his knees or flat onto the ground. While these scenarios do not always produce identical results, most opponents do react in this way. This is pivotal information for planning the Aiki-Jujutsu technique that might follow an attack. In addition to providing a momentary, painful distraction to an opponent, strikes are the first step in applying Kuzushi, directing an opponent's momentum to any direction (depending upon how a strike or series of strikes has affected the opponent). I urge you to choose your strikes carefully!

Uke Waza: Blocking Techniques

The blocking techniques of Fukasa-Ryu Kempo-Jutsu

are comprised of a combination of hand and leg deflections and body movements that have evasive and invasive characteristics. These techniques enable the martial artist to avoid or blend with an attack, positioning the body for a throw, joint-lock or sword-disarming technique of Aiki-Jujutsu.

Ude Ki Uke: Arm Internal Energy Block

I explained earlier that one of the axioms of Fukasa-Ryu Kempo-Jutsu is to *evade* an opposing force as opposed to *extinguish* it with a force of greater strength. This principle applies to all of the blocking techniques of the art, and it functions to produce blocks of a more 'passive' variety relative to other martial arts. Ude Ki Uke (arm internal energy block), for example, is performed with the arm positioned to the front of the side of the head and is not used to 'aggressively' deflect an incoming strike by smacking or pushing it out of the way. As the body is positioned to safely evade a strike or group of strikes, the arm is used to 'guard' a particular section of the body. In the case of a surprise attack, the block could be used to deflect a strike, thereby continuing the movement of the force yet signalling the opponent that he needs to change his game plan. This manoeuvre would be counterproductive if the objective was to grab an opponent's arms in order to perform a throw. However, such an objective would conflict with one of the basic tenants of the art, 'Ju', which means subtlety and gentleness (as in

Aiki-Jujutsu). A block, if it is to be successful, should be performed in a fashion that is almost undetectable to the opponent, with the result that he *thinks* he has been successful in his attack or realizes too late that he has failed to alter his course.

The manner in which Ki is used to block an opponent's attack, in lieu of the use of muscle power alone, is another distinguishing 'passive' characteristic of the blocks of this art. Employing Ude Ki Uke as an example, the muscles of the shoulder and arm are *only slightly tensed* in order to prevent the arm from ricocheting into the body during a block. The arm is otherwise held *completely relaxed*, using visualization and breathing techniques to direct the body's Ki toward the arm for empowerment.

Hidari Ude Ki Uke: Left Arm Internal Energy Block

Hidari Ude Ki Uke (left arm internal energy block) is used to block and position the body to the inside of an opponent's right arm in response to a right, straight or roundhouse attack. It is also used to block and position the body to the outside of an opponent's left arm in response to a straight attack.

Hidari Ude Ki Uke is performed from Hidari Hanmi Dachi by elevating the left arm and positioning it vertically at the front of the left side of the body. At the same time, the practitioner slides forward on the ball of the right foot, toward the right, oblique direction, situating into Migi Zenkutsu

Hidari Joden Ude Ki Uke.

Hidari Chuden Ude Ki Uke (against a right strike).

Block to strike.

Migi Chuden Ude Ki Uke (against a left strike).

Dachi (right forward stance). The left foot is drawn slightly forward in this direction because an elongated Zenkutsu Dachi can put the back leg (along with the rest of the body) at risk of being knocked backwards.

The left arm is bent at the elbow, and the forearm is held vertically in order to block the left side of the head and neck for Hidari Joden Ude Ki Uke (left upper-level arm internal energy block). To protect the left side of the ribcage, the elbow is positioned at a lower height, resting against the ribcage for Hidari Chuden Ude Ki Uke (left middle-level arm internal energy block).

In both cases, the fingers are held slightly bent and close together in a natural, relaxed fashion. This block can be used simultaneously with Migi Oi Tate Tsuki, creating a block and strike combination.

Migi Ude Ki Uke: Right Arm Internal Energy Block

Migi Ude Ki Uke (right arm internal energy block) is used to block and position the body to the inside of an opponent's left arm in response to a left, straight or roundhouse attack. It is also used to block and position the body to the outside of an opponent's right arm in response to a straight attack.

Migi Ude Ki Uke is performed from Hidari Hanmi Dachi by elevating the right arm and positioning it vertically at the front of the right side of the body. At the same time, the practitioner slides forward

Migi Joden Ude Ki Uke.

Migi Chuden Ude Ki Uke.

Block to strike.

on the ball of the left foot toward the left, oblique direction, situating into Hidari Zenkutsu Dachi (left forward stance). The right foot follows by being drawn slightly forward, similar to the fashion described in Hidari Ude Ki Uke. Migi Joden Ude Ki Uke (right upper-level arm internal energy block) is performed by positioning the right arm to protect the right side of the head and neck. Migi Chuden Ude Ki Uke (right middle-level arm internal energy block) is positioned at the level of the ribs to protect the side of the ribcage.

Similar to Hidari Ude Ki Uke, Hidari Oi Tate Tsuki (left vertical lunge punch) can be used in tandem with this block.

Teisho Uke: Palm Block

Similar to Ude Ki Uke, Teisho Uke (palm block) helps to guide or shield, rather than to forcefully deflect, a strike from hitting the body by combining an evasive movement of the body in tandem with the block. Dissimilar to Ude Ki Uke, which can be used to block attacks of both linear and 'round-house' varieties, Teisho Uke can only be used safely against a linear type of attack.

To use the block, the blocking hand must be open and bent all the way back at the wrist so the hand is positioned vertically, with the fingers and thumb pointed in an upward direction. The digits should be slightly bent, tightening the palm, and protecting the fingers and thumb from injury.

Migi Teisho Uke: Right Palm Block

To block and evade to the right side of a straight attack using Migi Teisho Uke, lift the open palm from the side of the body and direct it horizontally across the front of the body, from the right to the left side. Simultaneously slide the right foot forward to the front, right oblique direction in order to situate into Migi Zenkutsu Dachi. The height of the block should correlate with the height of the opponent's strike. Migi Joden Teisho Uke (right upper-level palm block) is a block that protects the head and neck areas of the body. Migi Chuden Teisho Uke (right middle-level palm block) is a block of this variety that protects the chest.

Migi Joden Teisho Uke.

Migi Chuden Teisho Uke.

Hidari Joden Teisho Uke.

Hidari Chuden Teisho Uke.

From Hidari Hanmi Dachi, Hidari Joden Teisho Uke (left upper-level palm block) and Hidari Chuden Teisho Uke (left middle-level palm block) are performed in the same manner as that described for the right hand, but now using the left foot to slide to the front, left, oblique direction, situating into Hidari Zenkutsu Dachi. The left block is used to block and move the body to the outside of an opponent's right, straight attack.

On both the right and left sides, it is always important to draw the back foot to a front oblique direction, situating into Zenkutsu Dachi, as opposed to elongating the stance by 'grounding' the back leg during a block, similar to Ude Ki Uke.

Hidari Gedan Barai Uke (against a right strike).

Gedan Barai Uke: Lower-Level Sweeping Block

Gedan Barai Uke (lower-level sweeping block) might be characterized as a deflecting, more aggressive type of blocking technique than blocks such as Ude Ki Uke and Teisho Uke. It is performed in tandem with a forward, oblique movement, so the technique is not entirely dependent upon the block's sweeping motion alone. The forward, oblique movement shifts the body out of harm's way, as the blocking arm sweeps or 'clears' the front of the body in order to protect against a linear strike to the ribs or gut.

Hidari Gedan Barai Uke: Left Lower-Level Sweeping Block

Hidari Gedan Barai Uke (left lower-level sweeping block) is performed, from Hidari Hanmi Dachi, by

circling the left arm in a vertical, clockwise motion in front of the body. Power for this block is generated from the forward motion of the body and the left shoulder and triceps. The fingers are relaxed and positioned fairly close together, with the thumb bent at the second knuckle, keeping the palm tense. The left side of the wrist intercepts the strike, directing it just beyond the left side of the body. The block finishes with the left hand positioned in line with the left leg, thereby diminishing the body's vulnerability to an attack. The palm faces downward, and the hand and arm are outstretched in a downward and outward, oblique direction.

In tandem with the blocking motion of the arm, the left foot slides to the front, left, oblique direction to assume Hidari Zenkutsu Dachi.

Hidari Gedan Barai Uke (step 1).

Hidari Gedan Barai Uke (step 2).

Hidari Gedan Barai Uke (finish).

Migi Gedan Barai Uke (against a left strike).

Hidari Gedan Te Uke.

Migi Gedan Te Uke.

Gedan Te Uke (against a right strike).

Migi Gedan Barai Uke: Right Lower-Level Sweeping Block

Migi Gedan Barai Uke is performed using the same footwork as Hidari Gedan Barai Uke to the front, left oblique direction. The block is done by sweeping the right hand in a vertical, counterclockwise direction at the front of the body.

Gedan Te Uke: Lower-Level Hand Block

Similar to Gedan Barai Uke, Gedan Te Uke is performed against a linear attack directed to the ribs or gut using identical footwork. The technique uses the palm of the hand, as opposed to the wrist, to block an opponent's attack.

To perform Hidari Gedan Te Uke (left lower-level hand block), the left hand is lifted from the left side of the body and arced downward in order to deflect an opponent's hand or wrist to that direction. The palm is tightened by bending the thumb and fingers slightly, and the hand is directed toward the right. Impact to the opponent's hand or wrist is made using the palm of the hand and is aimed at targeting an area close to the wrist.

Migi Gedan Te Uke (right lower-level hand block) is performed in exactly the same manner as the block using the left hand; the left foot slides to the same front, left, oblique direction to invade. Assume Hidari Zenkutsu Dachi.

Gedan Te Uke (against a left strike).

Ashi Uke: Leg Blocks

Ashi Uke (leg blocks) are used to protect the lower portion of the body, below the waist. They consist of knee and shin deflections and evasive movements that shift the body out of harm's way.

As a general rule, the Fukasa-Ryu style advocates that the practitioner use his hands to protect the upper quadrant of the body and his legs for protection of the lower quadrant of the body. Protection of the lower portion of the body, using the arms, requires that the back of the body is bent forward and that the arms are moved downward. While the hands are committed below this level, the face, neck and chest become vulnerable to an attack. This posture is also not optimal for the flow of Ki, which relies upon a straight back and a good posture in order to circulate around the body effectively. Furthermore, in a scenario in which the practitioner might have to defend against multiple attackers, the 'hunched over' posture would not allow for the mobility necessary to quickly respond to a myriad of different attacks. Quick, evasive movements would be the best choice to defend against the kicks of an opponent. Performing evasions requires minimal commitment of the hands or feet directed toward any single opponent and allows for the mobility and speed that is a necessity when faced with multiple opponents.

There are instances, however, when it might be necessary to use the legs to deflect an opponent's kick or strike to the lower portion of the body. If the practitioner were caught by surprise, for example, and attacked with a fury of multiple strikes to the front of the body, there might not be enough time to make an evasive movement in order to avoid getting hit. Knee and crane blocks might be effective in this type of scenario. Hiza Uke (knee block) is a very quick and effective technique to use against strikes that are targeted to areas below the level of the Hara. It can, however, only be used to protect the legs and groin.

Tsuru Uke (crane block) is a great alternative for strikes that are directed toward the upper leg, groin and abdominal (Hara) region. Caution should be exercised when using this type of block, however, because it is very easy to inadvertently fall off-

Ashi Uke (against an opponent).

balance while performing this technique, due to the fact that it requires the practitioner to stand on one leg. To minimize the likelihood of such an eventuality, the practitioner should spend as little time as possible on one leg. This can be accomplished by lifting the blocking leg into place just prior to the impact of the kick and resituating it back onto solid ground immediately following the block. In addition, I suggest that the leg that is used to block the opponent be positioned with its foot as low as possible against the shin area of the leg that supports the body. This allows for a swift return onto both feet.

The weight of the practitioner's body is directed slightly forward, so the impact of an opponent's attack gets rebounded to the direction from which it came and doesn't knock the practitioner's body back to the rear direction.

Tsuru Uke: Crane Leg Block

From Hidari Hanmi Dachi, shift the body's weight back onto the right leg, raise the left knee and position the sole of the left foot onto the right shin. Recover from the block by returning the left foot to the ground, lowering it forward into Hidari Hanmi Dachi. This will create a momentum to the front direction that can be used for a follow-up technique. Resettle into Hidari Hanmi Dachi if there is no reason to apply another technique.

During this technique, the hands can either stay relaxed at the sides of the body or move to the front of the body.

Tsuru Uke (against an opponent).

Hidari Hanmi Dachi.

Tsuru Uke (left block).

Hidari Hanmi Dachi.

Migi Hanmi Dachi.

Tsuru Uke (right block).

Tsuru Uke can also be performed using the right leg in a fashion similar to the method used while performing kicks. It is necessary, however, that the practitioner step back into Migi Hanmi Dachi if he desires to block using his right leg. Tsuru Uke is only effective when it is performed using the front leg because it protects the front of the body. In a combat scenario, Tsuru Uke might be performed subsequent to another technique that positions the body with the right leg forward.

Hiza Uke: Knee Block

Hiza Uke (knee block) is used to protect against low strikes directed to the legs and groin; both feet stay on the ground, so the body's balance is not compromised. From Hidari Hanmi Dachi, Hiza Uke is performed by simply twisting on the ball of the left foot. The twist can be used to deflect a strike using the knee, to avoid being hit by a strike directed at the knee or to direct the abdominal region and groin out of harm's way. In each scenario, the posi-

tion of the feet on the ground provides for a safe and swift transition back into Hidari Hanmi Dachi.

Hiza Uke can be performed with either the right or left leg, but the leg must be positioned at the front of the body to be effective, similar to Tsuru Uke. Performing this block using the back leg will

Hiza Uke (against an opponent).

Hidari Hanmi Dachi.

Hiza Uke (twist foot 1).

Hiza Uke (twist foot 2).

Shomen Uchi (ready position).

Shomen Uchi (swing blade back).

Shomen Uchi (swing blade downward).

'tie-up' the body and immobilize the legs, thereby making it impractical.

Evasive and Invasive Techniques Against the Sword

It is my opinion that the most efficacious method of self-protection against an attack from an opponent wielding any type of bladed weapon, assuming there are absolutely no other options but to handle a confrontation using physical force, is to use the breath in order to relax and to keep the limbs close to the body! Arms that are held to the front of the body risk debilitating slashes, while legs that are positioned in wide, deep stances do not afford the ability to make quick evasive or invasive movements in response to an attack. A narrow stance, utilized in tandem with evasive and invasive techniques, and without the use of blocks, is the safest method of defence against a bladed, weapon-wielding attacker.

Outside Evasions from a Shomen Uchi, Vertical Downward 'Head Cut' Attack

Evasion to the Left Side of a Shomen Uchi from Hidari Hanmi Dachi

As the blade begins to make its vertical descent toward the head, initiate a movement to the front, left oblique direction by sliding on the ball of the left foot and dragging on the ball of the right, back foot in order to resituate into Hidari Hanmi Dachi. This positions the body to the left of the blade. Follow by striking the opponent to the left side of the chin using Hidari Yoko Empi Uchi (left side elbow strike). This is performed by sliding the left foot toward the opponent, assuming Hidari Zenkutsu Dachi for power.

Hidari Hanmi Dachi (against an opponent).

Evasion to the Right Side of a Shomen Uchi from Hidari Hanmi Dachi

As the blade begins to make its vertical descent toward the head, initiate a movement to the front, right, oblique direction by sliding on the ball of the back, right foot and dragging on the ball of the left foot in order to resituate into Migi Hanmi Dachi.

This positions the body to the right of the blade. Follow by striking the opponent to the right side of the chin using Migi Yoko Empi Uchi (right side elbow strike). This is performed by sliding the right foot toward the opponent, ending in Migi Zenkutsu Dachi.

Evasion to left oblique.

Hidari Yoko Empi Uchi (elbow strike).

Evasion to right oblique.

Migi Yoko Empi Uchi (elbow strike).

Hidari Hanmi Dachi (against an opponent).

Straight invasion (against a Shomen Uchi).

Pre-Emptive, Straight Invasion Against a Shomen Uchi from Hidari Hanmi Dachi

As the opponent cocks the blade overhead to prepare for the Shomen Uchi, use the right foot to rapidly advance forward toward the opponent as his arms are raised. Assume Migi Zenkutsu Dachi to block the opponent's arms from swinging the blade forward. Block against the underside of the opponent's forearms using the right forearm positioned above and to the front of the head at a 45-degree angle. Position the left arm higher and at the oppo-site angle in order to block the opponent's right arm with the wrist. According to the throwing technique to follow, either off-balance the opponent to his rear or strike the opponent to his front, using your legs to off-balance him.

Straight Evasion to the Rear from Hidari Hanmi Dachi Against a Gyaku Age Uchi Attack (Reverse Diagonal Rising Cut)

As the blade begins to ascend from the left side of the opponent's body, use the right, back foot

Hidari Hanmi Dachi (against an opponent).

Straight evasion (against Gyaku Age Uchi).

Straight evasion (finish).

Migi Gedan Oi Tate Tsuki (follow-up technique).

to initiate a slide directly to the rear. Retreat into Hidari Hanmi Dachi, moving the body just beyond the sword's reach. After the sword passes by, use the right foot to advance straight forward and grab the opponent's right wrist using your left hand. Follow with a quick strike to the opponent's ribs using Migi Gedan Oi Tate Tsuki (right lower-level vertical lunging fist strike) in Migi Zenkutsu Dachi.

Note: if, at the conclusion of the cut, the sword's tip is positioned beyond the front of the opponent's body, it will be necessary to advance forward in a slight, right, oblique direction in order to avoid colliding with the tip of the blade.

Straight Evasion to the Rear from Hidari Hanmi Dachi Against a Nuki Dashi Age (Rising Oblique Sword Draw)

This evasion is performed in exactly the same manner as the evasion from a Gyaku Age Uchi attack, the only noticeable difference being that, in this case, the opponent will be holding the sword with one hand.

Hidari Hanmi Dachi (against an opponent).

Straight evasion (against Nuki Dashi Age).

Grab wrist.

Migi Gedan Oi Tate Tsuki (follow-up technique).

Pre-Emptive, Straight Invasion from Hidari Hanmi Dachi Against a Nuki Dashi Age (Rising Oblique Sword Draw) or Nuki Dashi Tomoe (Stomach-Level Sword Draw)

As the opponent's hand reaches to grab the hilt of his sword in order to execute the draw, use your right foot to rapidly advance straight ahead toward the opponent. Assume Migi Zenkutsu Dachi and intercept the draw with the left, open hand by pressing the opponent's right wrist back toward his body. Use Migi Reiken Uchi (right back knuckle strike) in order to quickly strike the opponent's nose. These measures will surely prevent the opponent from unsheathing his sword.

Hidari Hanmi Dachi (against an opponent).

Straight invasion and strike.

PART III

AIKI-JUJUTSU: BODY-CONDITIONING TECHNIQUES

Now that I have described techniques that enable the practitioner to move within 'arms reach' of an opponent, let us take a look at some Aiki-Jujutsu techniques that are essential prerequisites to learning how to throw an opponent. Ukemi (which includes falling and rolling techniques), Tai Sabaki (body turning) and Shikko Waza (knee-walking) are all techniques that fall into this category.

CHAPTER 4

UKEMI WAZA: BREAK-FALLING TECHNIQUES

Ukemi Waza (break-falling techniques) protect the Aiki-Jujutsu-Ka or practitioner of any throwing art from the perils associated with being thrown by an opponent. In order to minimize the chance of bodily injury, the body is relaxed and the mind is calm and free of fear. As the practitioner's body impacts to the Tatame, it does so gracefully, without the burden of being tense, thus avoiding injury. I am not implying that the practitioner 'leave things in the hands of the Tori (thrower)' and allow the opponent to send him careening through the air onto the Tatame. An Uki (faller) must focus on positioning himself correctly during a fall in order to protect his limbs from breaking upon impact to the mat. In the event that a throw entailing a wrist or arm-locking technique has 'motivated' an Uki to flip as a result of the pain that has been inflicted upon his limbs, he must propel himself into an aerial break-fall in order to escape injury. The Uki must be focused and quick at responding to the whims of his opponent, if he should be forced to fall without choice.

Many spectators of the combat-oriented throwing arts seem to believe that the combatants are merely 'putting on a show' by jumping into the air in an effort to make their partners and the martial art look effective and beautiful. Let me assure you that this is *not* the case! Let me state for the record that students of the Fukasa-Ryu style are instructed to do otherwise and to use break-falling techniques and rolls only as a vehicle to (1) protect their limbs from breaking on impact to the Tatame, or (2) to escape a wrist or arm-locking technique when there is no other option. The practitioner should yield to pain and momentum if he reacts too slowly to counter a technique or movement. A hesitation or

late response might not only be ineffective at such a late point in a technique, it also signals to the opponent that you have caught on to his 'game-plan'. This usually results in an additional response or 'change of plan' by the opponent – a change that the practitioner might not be prepared to handle. Under this circumstance, the practitioner should yield and merely 'Be', accepting that he's been succumbed by a technique. Protect yourself by falling or rolling in a direction that will alleviate the pain of a lock and protect the rest of the body. If an aerial break-fall might be necessary to escape the hazards of an arm or wristlock, you are ahead of it by jumping over it or rolling out of it.

Observers of this type of defence frequently get the wrong idea about this strategy because they fail to understand the logic behind a tactic that prompts a practitioner to 'flip' out of a technique. In addition, an Uki, in order to adjust the angle of his body so that he falls properly and escapes injury from a wild, uncontrolled throw, might opt to propel himself higher in the air than would appear to be necessary. Please note, however, that an additional benefit of this pre-emptive, extra-high break-fall (especially for males) is that the severity of the impact to the genitalia is significantly reduced. In summation, an Uki must be proactive in relaxing, exhaling, propelling and angling the body correctly during a throw in order to protect his limbs and maximize the 'comfort-level' of the fall.

Ushiro Ukemi: Rear Break-Fall

From Hidari Hanmi Dachi, 'lock' your chin to your

Hidari Hanmi Dachi.

Ushiro Ukemi (cross arms, right foot forward).

Ushiro Ukemi (bend knees).

Ushiro Ukemi (slap the mat).

and forefingers slightly, keeping them close together and tighten the palms; the latter will impact with the Tatame along with the forearms. Lift the right leg straight up in the front of the body, with the knee straightened. Lower the buttocks onto the Tatame with your left leg raised next to the right leg at approximately a 90-degree angle relative to the Tatame. As the lower portion of your back makes its impact on the Tatame, slap, using the outer edge of the palms below the ring and pinky fingers and make sure to keep the arms at a 45-degree angle relative to the body. This will 'break' the fall, protecting the back of your body from most of the impact.

Relax the body and allow gravity to guide the legs downward, beyond the front of the body. Bend the knees and 'fold' the right leg below the left leg, positioning it perpendicular to the left leg, with the right foot pointing to the left direction. Recover by rising onto the right knee. Prepare the right leg

chest in order to stabilize the head for impact and slide your right foot forward. Bend the left knee and, with the hands open, lift both arms in front of the body, crossing them at the wrists. Bend the thumbs to stand by twisting it counterclockwise on the right kneecap and extend the right leg back so that its weight rests on the ball of the foot. Finish by standing into Hidari Hanmi Dachi.

Ushiro Ukemi (fold the leg).

Ushiro Ukemi (prepare to stand).

Hidari Hanmi Dachi (finish).

Hidari Hanmi Dachi.

Migi Yoko Ukemi (hand ready, slide forward, chin down).

Migi Yoko Ukemi (bend).

Migi Yoko Ukemi (slap the mat).

Migi Yoko Ukemi (fold leg).

Migi Yoko Ukemi (recover and prepare to stand).

Yoko Ukemi: Side Break-Fall

Migi Yoko Ukemi: Right Side Break-Fall
Migi Yoko Ukemi (right side break-fall) is performed in almost the exact manner as described for Ushiro Ukemi. However, the body makes contact with the Tatame on its right side rather than on the whole of the back. The left hand has no function during this break-fall and just hangs relaxed at the left side of the body.

Hidari Yoko Ukemi: Left Side Break-Fall
Hidari Yoko Ukemi (left side break-fall) is similar to Migi Yoko Ukemi, and is only performed from Migi Hanmi Dachi (*see* Chapter 3). It cannot be performed from Hidari Hanmi Dachi, so the practitioner must adjust his posture by shifting his right foot forward *before* a throw, should he believe that

Hidari Hanmi Dachi (finish).

Migi Hanmi Dachi.

Hidari Yoko Ukemi (hand ready, slide forward, chin down).

Hidari Yoko Ukemi (bend).

Hidari Yoko Ukemi (slap the mat).

Hidari Yoko Ukemi (prepare to fold the leg).

Hidari Yoko Ukemi (fold leg).

Hidari Yoko Ukemi (rise onto the knee).

Migi Hanmi Dachi (finish).

Mae Chugaeri: Front Somersault Break-Fall

Mae Chugaeri (front somersault break-fall) might be performed if a practitioner found himself being thrown straight over an opponent's shoulders or if he needed to protect his arms from breaking by somersaulting over them. Either manoeuvre could result in the practitioner falling flat onto the back of his body.

From Hidari Hanmi Dachi, slide the right foot forward to assume Migi Hanmi Dachi. Lift both arms, crossing them at the wrists, with both hands at about the level of the forehead. The hands are held open, with the thumbs and fingers bent slightly and spaced in

he is about to be thrown onto his left side. Otherwise the positioning of the body will not correlate with the break-fall and may result in injury to the body.

Mae Chugaeri (slide forward, lift and cross arms).

Mae Chugaeri (spring upward).

Mae Chugaeri (flip 1).

Mae Chugaeri (flip 2).

Mae Chugaeri (slap the mat).

Mae Chugaeri (feet landing on the mat).

close proximity to one another. This is done in order to tighten the palms and protect the fingers from separating upon impact.

To launch into the somersault, the legs are bent at the knees and ankles in order to spring upward. Jump by straightening the knees and flexing the ankles, thereby flipping the body upside down. Using the arms to slap down, land on the back of the body. As the balls of both feet touch the ground, the knees are bent to absorb the impact to the legs. Begin the jump by swinging both arms forcefully downward toward the rear of the body, while tucking the chin deeply into the chest. Use a quick, snapping movement to create a vertical, circular motion for the somersault, thus propelling the body into a forward rotation. Maintain the head at a stable height as the feet (and legs) rise up and fly over the head from the rear, inverting the body 360 degrees.

During the somersault, the back is kept as straight as possible in order to eliminate the risk of falling prematurely, hitting the head and possibly injuring other parts of the body. The arms, which helped to create the body's forward rotation, are used to break the fall in a manner that is similar to the way in which they are used in Ushiro Ukemi. In this case, however, the legs also play a role in softening the body's landing. As the balls of both feet impact upon the Tatame, the knees are bent and the legs are separated in order to prevent them from colliding. Subsequent to the fall, rise into Hidari Hanmi Dachi in the manner described in Ushiro Ukemi. As a general rule, during break-falling, the practitioner inhales deeply through the nose just prior to a fall and forcefully exhales from the mouth the moment the body impacts upon the Tatame. This proactive release of air prevents the uncomfortable, involuntary exhale that usually occurs as a result of being inadequately prepared to fall.

In the more advanced student levels of Fukasa-Ryu Aiki-Jujutsu, disciples are expected to perform somersault break-falls without using any portion of their arms to 'break the fall'. An advanced student of Ukemi, who is performing a Mae Chugaeri, should have the ability to adjust his body position in the air so that he falls flat onto the Tatame with the balls of the feet taking most of the impact of the fall. No discomfort in the back of the body should be experienced. This might appear to be counter-intuitive since I had suggested that, at the most fundamental level, the arms are the primary means through which a fall is broken. The comfort-level of the landing, however, almost entirely depends upon the body's orientation at the moment of impact and is most critical when the arms are not used to break the fall.

Yoko Chugaeri: Side Somersault Break-Fall

Yoko Chugaeri (side somersault break-fall) is used if an opponent throws his body sideways (as opposed to straight) into a fall, resulting in the body landing on its side. This technique, similar to Mae Chugaeri, is also a means by which to escape an arm or wristlock.

Migi Yoko Chugaeri: Right Side Somersault Break-Fall

From Hidari Hanmi Dachi (see Chapter 3), slide the right foot forward into Migi Hanmi Dachi. Slightly bend the knees and ankles in order to prepare for a somersault. Circle the right arm vertically, back and up from the right side of the body, so it almost completes one rotation and ends positioned to the front, right side of the body in the area of the ribcage. Tuck the chin deeply into the chest and flip the body over in a manner similar to the method used in Mae Chugaeri.

Unlike Mae Chugaeri, the chest faces toward the front, left, oblique direction so that the left side of the body lands on the Tatame. Just prior to the somersault, however, the practitioner directs his vision forward, while the right foot points straight ahead similar to Migi Hanmi Dachi. Inadvertently directing the right foot toward the left direction can cause the body to veer off to that direction during the somersault. The practitioner must propel himself straight over, directly to the front of the body.

When the side of the body impacts with the Tatame, the left arm is used to slap, in a manner similar to Hidari Yoko Ukemi. The legs land onto the mat with the left leg straight, positioned to the side, while the right leg is

Migi Yoko Chugaeri (slide forward).

Migi Yoko Chugaeri (circle arm).

Migi Yoko Chugaeri (flip).

Migi Yoko Chugaeri (slap the mat).

Hidari Yoko Chugaeri (slide forward).   *Hidari Yoko Chugaeri (flip).*   *Hidari Yoko Chugaeri (slap the mat).*

positioned so that it rests on the ball of the foot. The left foot is bent forward at the ankles, thus enabling the toes to be straightened so that the foot, heel and ankles do not hit the Tatame on the fall. The right leg, with the knee bent, lands in a vertical orientation so there is less of a chance that both legs will collide during the fall. Rock slightly to the rear direction, positioning the body's weight onto the whole of the back. Bend the left leg at the knee in order to fold it horizontally below the right leg. This position permits the practitioner to rock forward and rise onto the left knee. Finish by standing into Migi Hanmi Dachi.

Hidari Yoko Chugaeri: Left Side Somersault Break-Fall

Hidari Yoko Chugaeri (left side somersault break-fall) is performed in the same manner as Migi Yoko Chugaeri. In order to create a momentum for the somersault, assume Migi Hanmi Dachi and step forward into Hidari Hanmi Dachi.

A note regarding the use of Chugaeri during actual throws: during an actual throw, there will not always be an opportunity to take a step forward in order to create a momentum for a somersault; this is mostly used for solo practice. Prior to being thrown, it is absolutely imperative that the practitioner's foot position, with the legs aligned correctly, corresponds to the side of the body that will allow for a safe impact onto the Tatame. Additionally, if the practitioner's stance is incongruent with the way his body is being manipulated for a throw, there is less of a chance that he can pre-emptively propel

himself over quickly enough to protect his limbs from breaking due to an opponent's wrist-locking or arm-breaking throwing technique.

Hip throws that do not have a wrist-locking or arm-breaking element do not necessarily require the use of a Chugaeri, but in order to prevent injury to the legs as the body impacts onto the Tatame, hip throws do require the same leg configuration performed using a Chugaeri.

Mae Ukemi: Front Break-Fall

Mae Ukemi (front break-fall) protects the front of the body from injury if the practitioner should find himself falling forward onto the front of his body. In my opinion, it is one of the most practical falling techniques. I am certain that just about everyone has had the experience of inadvertently tripping on something that resulted in a fall to a forward direction. The instinctive human response is to stop a fall by putting the hands forward to protect the front of the body from hitting the ground. However, depending upon the speed of the fall and the type of surface on which the fall occurs, this may lead to injury of the hands and elbows.

Mae Ukemi can be performed from Hidari Hanmi Dachi. Protect the chest by positioning the arms at the front of the body, resting the elbows tightly against the upper ribcage, with the inside of the forearms and open palms directed to the front by twisting the wrists. Turn the head to either the left or right direction in order to protect the nose and front of the face from impacting onto the Tatame. Slide the feet back to opposite, rear, oblique directions, straightening the knees and spreading the legs wide so that the landing is accomplished with the body's weight resting on the balls of the feet. Fall forward, allowing the upper body to make contact with the Tatame on the forearms and palms. The fingers of the hands are held tightly together, with the thumb bent back, tensing the palm.

Be certain that the elbows are positioned close to one another, with the arms forming a 'V' shape, pointing to opposite, oblique directions at the front of the body. The legs, forming a 'V' shape and pointed to opposite, oblique directions to the rear, are spread as widely apart as possible, with the lower portion of the body resting comfortably on the balls of the feet. The legs are 'locked' straight at the knees in order to protect them (i.e. the knees) from injury; the knees should never make contact with the Tatame. It is important, with regard to any type of break-falling technique, that the practitioner exhale through his mouth just as the body impacts onto the Tatame. This will increase the comfort-level of the fall and allow for a smoother recovery into the next technique.

An After-Thought Regarding Ukemi

The practitioner should make a conscious effort to keep the head stabilized throughout the duration of any falling technique. In general, keep the head away from the Tatame and try to protect it from jolting to any direction in order to prevent whiplash to the neck.

The break-falls that I have demonstrated in this book require the use of the forearms and palms to strike the Tatame. It is important to attempt to 'lock' the elbow, as the fall is broken, with the slap. Other styles of Bujutsu advocate a light 'tap' to the Tatame in order to follow with a rapid recovery into some type of defensive guard. While this is a good idea, never do this prematurely. Since the practitioner's first concern as an Uki is to protect his body from injury during a fall, it is my recommendation that he strike the Tatame with a committed and powerful blow!

Hidari Hanmi Dachi.

Mae Ukemi (position arms and turn head).

Mae Ukemi (fall and thrust legs back).

Mae Ukemi (finish).

CHAPTER 5

ROTARY ROLLS, KNEE WALKING AND BODY PIVOTS

Rotary rolls are used in Aiki-Jujutsu if the practitioner finds himself projected forward with great momentum. To avoid the possibly of tripping off-balance or awkwardly trying to regain the body's stability, rotary rolls enable the Aiki-Jujutsu-Ka to tumble smoothly and quickly away from his opponent's follow-up technique. In addition, they allow for a swift recovery into a combat-ready posture at a safe distance from an opponent, allowing for some extra time to face an opponent with a clear mind.

Mae Zempo Kaiten: Front Rotary Roll

Migi Mae Zempo Kaiten: Right Front Rotary Roll

Prepare for Migi Mae Zempo Kaiten (right front rotary roll) by sliding the right foot forward from Hidari Hanmi Dachi (see Chapter 3) into a deep posture, with the left knee bent deeply and the foot resting on its ball. Circle the right arm vertically, back and up from the right side of the body, positioning it arced beyond the front of the body. The right elbow and wrist are bent slightly and the palm is directed toward the Tatame, with the fingers held close together, pointing toward the left direction. Tuck the chin into the chest and keep the eyes focused straight ahead, beyond the front of the body.

Tumble forward by pushing off of both legs in order to make contact with the Tatame on the area of the arm located just above the outside of the wrist bone. As the body rolls over, contact with the mat is made at the upper right arm, across the back of the right shoulder, and diagonally across from the upper, right corner of the back, down to the left, lower portion of the back. Recover from the roll by folding the left leg under the right leg, similar to the manner described for Hidari Yoko Ukemi (see Chapter 4). Stand and shift the right leg back into Hidari Hanmi Dachi to assume the original start position.

Hidari Hanmi Dachi.

Migi Mae Zempo Kaiten (circle arm).

Migi Mae Zempo Kaiten (bend knees).

*Migi Mae Zempo Kaiten
(roll forward 1).*

*Migi Mae Zempo Kaiten
(roll forward 2).*

*Migi Mae Zempo Kaiten
(roll forward 3).*

*Migi Mae Zempo Kaiten
(begin to fold leg).*

*Migi Mae Zempo Kaiten
(leg folded).*

*Migi Mae Zempo Kaiten
(preparing to stand).*

Hidari Hanmi Dachi (finish).

*Hidari Mae Zempo Kaiten
(slide foot and circle arm).*

*Hidari Mae Zempo Kaiten
(fold leg to recover).*

*Hidari Mae Zempo Kaiten
(preparing to stand).*

Hidari Hanmi Dachi (finish).

Hidari Mae Zempo Kaiten:
Left Front Rotary Roll

Hidari Mae Zempo Kaiten (left front rotary roll) is performed in a fashion similar to Migi Mae Zempo Kaiten from Migi Hanmi Dachi (see Chapter 3). Stand and recover directly into Hidari Hanmi Dachi or, if the resumption of the original start position is desired, shift the left foot back to assume Migi Hanmi Dachi.

In order to employ either a roll or falling technique, the practitioner must be mindful that the legs must be adjusted to a position that facilitates 'yielding' to an opponent's throw. Just prior to a throw, an Uki pre-emptively adjusts his feet so the foot that is forward correlates with the arm that the Tori is using to perform the throw. If this is disregarded, the body and legs might be misaligned and this will hamper the ability to roll or fall in a safe and efficient manner.

Some of the more advanced throwing techniques of Fukasa-Ryu Aiki-Jujutsu utilize two arms to throw an opponent, while other throws are intended to be used to throw opponents who are situated in reverse postures, postures where the arms and legs have an inverse relationship. In these situations, an Uki must come to a quick and resolute decision as to which leg to position forward and to which direction he needs to tilt his airborne body, so that he might be able to roll or fall with an injury-free landing. Such successful spontaneity results only from many hours of falling practice with a partner. Being a great Uki is truly an admirable art and skill.

Ushiro Zempo Kaiten: Rear Rotary Roll

Ushiro Zempo Kaiten (rear rotary roll) can be employed if the practitioner finds himself being pushed from the front of the body to the rear direction with sufficient force that he has enough momentum to roll over backwards.

Ushiro Zempo Kaiten capitalizes on the speed of a projection-type throwing technique, flipping the body over and recovering by standing directly into Hanmi Dachi, the combat-ready position.

Hidari Ushiro Zempo Kaiten: Left Rear Rotary Roll

From Hidari Hanmi Dachi (see Chapter 3), direct the right foot across to the left, beyond the back of

Hidari Ushiro Zempo Kaiten (cross legs).

Hidari Ushiro Zempo Kaiten (bend knees).

Hidari Ushiro Zempo Kaiten (spring upward).

Hidari Ushiro Zempo Kaiten (drop and fold leg).

Hidari Ushiro Zempo Kaiten (roll backwards 1).

Hidari Ushiro Zempo Kaiten (roll backwards 2).

Hidari Ushiro Zempo Kaiten (roll backwards 3).

Hidari Ushiro Zempo Kaiten (finish roll).

Hidari Ushiro Zempo Kaiten (recover and prepare to stand).

the left foot, as if to assume Hidari Kosa Dachi (left cross stance) (see Chapter 3), and jump upward in place. Land on the left foot and lower the body's weight gradually, allowing the right leg to fold horizontally to the left direction as the buttocks drop toward the Tatame.

Stabilize the head by tucking the chin tightly onto the top of the chest. Swing the legs upward and over the left shoulder, keeping them together and straight at the knees. The arms hang relaxed at the sides of the body throughout the course of the roll. After rolling over, recover by standing directly into Hidari Hanmi Dachi. To escape injury to the neck and to prevent dizziness, be sure to direct both legs over the shoulder, as opposed to directing them straight over the head.

Migi Ushiro Zempo Kaiten (Right Rear Rotary Roll)

This is executed in a similar manner when it is performed from Migi Hanmi Dachi.

Shikko Waza: Knee-Walking Techniques

Shikko Waza (knee-walking techniques) were used by the Samurai to move stealthily, close to the ground, below the normal field of view. In order to wage a sneak attack or to disappear quickly, they might have used the techniques to move quickly alongside a fence or shrubs, to appear or disappear, having moved a great distance on their knees.

Migi Hanmi Dachi.

Migi Ushiro Zempo Kaiten (cross legs).

Migi Ushiro Zempo Kaiten (spring upward).

Migi Ushiro Zempo Kaiten (drop and fold leg).

Migi Ushiro Zempo Kaiten (roll backwards 1).

Migi Ushiro Zempo Kaiten (roll backwards 2).

Migi Ushiro Zempo Kaiten (recover and prepare to stand).

Migi Hanmi Dachi (finish).

A Samurai might have employed Shikko Waza to quickly move from a relaxed, seated position (Seiza), if he found himself under attack while eating or resting. Shikko Waza has an important role with respect to the throwing techniques of Fukasa-Ryu Aiki-Jujutsu, which can almost all be performed from the kneeling and standing positions.

From Hidari Hanmi Dachi, while dropping onto the right knee and the ball of the right foot, slap the right portion of the Hakama between the legs, so that it pops through to the outside of the right leg. Slap the remaining portion of the Hakama below and to the outside of the left leg in a similar way and lower the buttocks onto the heels of both feet. This should situate the body into Han-Sankyo, a kneeling position, with one knee positioned on the Tatame to an oblique, front direction (carrying the majority

Hidari Han-Sankyo.

Left knee down.

Migi Han-Sankyo.

Right knee down.

Hidari Han-Sankyo.

of the body's weight) and the other knee positioned off the Tatame, directed forward.

Because the technique began from Hidari Hanmi Dachi, assume Hidari Han-Sankyo with the left knee pointed to the front, positioned off the Tatame and the right knee situated to a right, oblique direction, the knee positioned on the Tatame.

The momentum for the knee-walk is created by a combination of a twisting motion of the hips and the body's upper torso. The hands are aligned to the front and centre of the body, approximating the level of the stomach. The palms face outward and the fingers point directly forward.

To begin knee-walking from Hidari Han-Sankyo, the left knee gently drops into position on the Tatame, transferring the body's weight onto the knee. The upper torso twists in a counterclockwise direction, enabling the right knee to move to the front position, off the Tatame, into Migi Han-Sankyo.

To continue the forward momentum of the body, drop the right knee to position it gently onto the Tatame, rotate the upper-torso and hips in a clockwise direction, and shift the left knee off the Tatame, into the front position

Be mindful to simultaneously adjust and coordinate the position of the hands from the rear to the front position. The hand changes not only guard the front of the body, but they can help to facilitate the body to twist and generate a forward momentum. There is a converse relationship between the movement of the hands and legs. So, for example, if the right hand and right knee are situated at the front position at the beginning of a knee movement, they should move to the rear position as the left knee and hand move forward.

Shikko Waza should always be performed on the balls of the feet. The feet move together within close proximity of each other. Separating the feet during knee-walking decreases the ability to twist, diminishing the momentum of the knee-walk.

Special attention should also be focused on the manner in which the knees make contact with the Tatame before they twist forward, adjusting the posture. Dropping the body's weight onto the knees too quickly can cause the knees to sustain injury as they impact onto the Tatame. In view of the vulnerability of the knees when they are subjected to these moves over an extended period of time, it is suggested that the practitioner understand well the mechanism of the knees in the execution of Shikko Waza.

Tai Sabaki: Body Pivots

Tai Sabaki are performed repetitively as routine,

warm-up exercises that allow the Aiki-Jujutsu-Ka to practise the foot-stepping techniques used to enter into the 'throwing position'. These exercises condition the body for a smooth, uninhibited and continuous flowing movement that simulates the steps of the evasive and invasive foot movements of Kempo-Jutsu. These exercises focus on footwork, body alignment and the achievement of balanced posture, the prerequisites for a good throw.

Wazari Tai Sabaki: Half-Body Pivot

From Hidari Hanmi Dachi (see Chapter 3), the left foot shuffles back slightly on the ball of the foot and then slides forward approximately 12 inches (30cm). The right foot skips forward about 3 feet (1m) by springing off of the left foot. The left foot immediately follows by shifting forward to a right, oblique direction and is now positioned behind and to the right of the right foot. Assume Migi Kosa Dachi (see Chapter 3).

As the body leaps into this position, the hands are lifted from the sides and positioned to the front of the body, with the right hand to the front of the left hand, similar to the way in which they were demonstrated to move in the kicking techniques included this book (see Chapter 3, Geri Waza).

Recover into Hidari Hanmi Dachi by sliding the left foot diagonally back, in line with its original position. Move the right foot straight back to the rear direction, drawing the left foot back slightly more, to the rear direction. The right hand moves behind the left hand, correlating with the movement of the legs and then drops down to the sides of the body as the body resettles into Hidari Hanmi Dachi.

Wazari Tai Sabaki is performed from Migi Hanmi Dachi in a similar fashion. From this stance, the legs skip forward into Hidari Kosa Dachi and then recover back into Migi Hanmi Dachi.

Special attention should be placed on 'grounding' the body into a deep and balanced Kosa Dachi after the hands have moved into the guard position at the front of the body. In addition, the

Hidari Hanmi Dachi.

Wazari Tai Sabaki (slide forward).

Wazari Tai Sabaki (cross stance).

Wazari Tai Sabaki.

Wazari Tai Sabaki (slide back).

Hidari Hanmi Dachi (finish).

Migi Hanmi Dachi.

Wazari Tai Sabaki (slide forward).

Wazari Tai Sabaki (cross stance).

Wazari Tai Sabaki.

Wazari Tai Sabaki (slide back).

Migi Hanmi Dachi (finish).

practitioner should not permit his chest to over-rotate to either the right or left direction when assuming Kosa Dachi. The chest is positioned to the front, oblique direction in this posture. This particular Tai Sabaki represents a manner in which a practitioner might enter into the inside of a strike in order to position himself for a throwing technique to the front of an opponent's body.

Ippon Tai Sabaki: Full Body Pivot

Ippon Tai Sabaki (full body pivot) enables a practitioner to evade an opponent's attack by moving to the outside of it, around the body of the opponent, and into a throw causing the opponent to fall to the rear direction.

From Hidari Hanmi Dachi (see Chapter 3), commence the forward movement in a similar fashion to Wazari Tai Sabaki by shuffling the left foot in preparation for a slide forward. Simultaneously extend both arms straight out beyond the right side of the body at about the level of the

chest. The arms are used to balance the body and to generate a twisting momentum similar to the way a helicopter's propellers rotate. Slide the left foot forward and twist the body 360 degrees in

Hidari Hanmi Dachi.

Ippon Tai Sabaki (arms ready).

Ippon Tai Sabaki (twist 1).

Ippon Tai Sabaki (twist 2).

Ippon Tai Sabaki (twist 3).

Ippon Tai Sabaki (twist 4).

Ippon Tai Sabaki (slide forward).

Ippon Tai Sabaki (cross stance).

Ippon Tai Sabaki (slide back).

Hidari Hanmi Dachi (finish).

a counter-clockwise direction by allowing the right foot to slide and position itself to the front of the left foot. Continue the turn by twisting on the ball of the right foot in order to slide the left foot to the original, front position, completing the rotation. Without stopping the body's momentum, slide the right foot forward once more and situate the left foot behind and to the right direction to assume Migi Kosa Dachi. Recover in the same manner as demonstrated in Wazari Tai Sabaki. Slide the left foot to the rear, left, oblique direction followed by a straight movement of the right foot to the rear position, drawing the left foot back slightly more to the rear direction, recovering into Hidari Hanmi Dachi.

Ippon Tai Sabaki is performed symmetrically from Migi Hanmi Dachi.

Migi Hanmi Dachi.

Ippon Tai Sabaki (arms ready).

Ippon Tai Sabaki (twist 1).

Ippon Tai Sabaki (twist 2).

Ippon Tai Sabaki (twist 3).

Ippon Tai Sabaki (slide forward).

Ippon Tai Sabaki (cross stance).

Ippon Tai Sabaki (slide back).

Migi Hanmi Dachi (finish).

PART IV

FUKASA-RYU AIKI-JUJUTSU

Proper breath control, visualization and correct posture work synergistically to cata-lyse the movement of Ki, greatly influencing the outcome of a throw. The efficacy of striking techniques is also dependent upon the student's ability to harness and channel Ki at the appropriate time. For most throwing techniques, the index finger is used to channel energy to a particular direction in order to guide an opponent easily into a throw, using the practitioner's internal energy or 'Ki'. This technique minimizes the use of the practitioner's muscular force. The index finger does not function to grip the arm of the opponent that is being used to off-balance him; in most instances, it is held straight, pointed to the direction in which the opponent will be forced to go.

The natural environment by which we are surrounded is comprised entirely of Ki… the Sun, Air, Water and Earth provide the earth's inhabitants with the 'force' or Ki that fosters life as we know it. If we can harness the energy around us 'on-demand', assimilate it into our own internal Ki and then project it outward via technique, we have manifested the essence of 'Aiki'. The application of 'Aiki' to the art of Jujutsu (Aiki-Jujtusu) does not have an exclusive on this concept. We can apply this concept to virtu-ally anything we do in life. Jigoro Kano, one of the world's most famous Jujutsu-Ka, who, at only 22 years of age created his style of Judo, used this idea as the foundation for his system. In doing so, he clearly demonstrated unusual insight for an individual of his age.

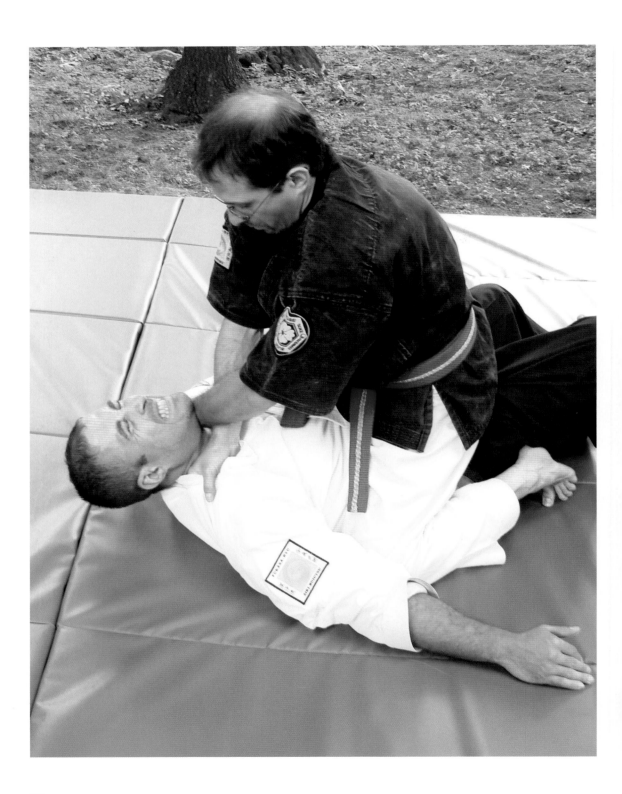

CHAPTER 6

AIKI NAGE WAZA: THROWING TECHNIQUES FROM SAMURAI SWORD AND WEAPONS-FREE ATTACKS

Aiki Sei Otoshi: Shoulder Drop

Aiki Sei Otoshi can be performed from the inside of a straight or roundhouse strike that emanates from an opponent's right or left hand. From an attack by the opponent's right hand, the practitioner evades to the right, forward, oblique direction using Hidari Ude Ki Uke and uses his right hand to perform Migi Gedan Oi Tate Tsuki (right lower-level vertical lunging fist strike) to the opponent's ribs. Kuzushi or 'off-balancing' is created, resulting in a slight weight imbalance of the opponent's body, causing him to fall forward. The practitioner draws the opponent further in this direction by using his left hand to grab the top of the opponent's right wrist and pulling his arm forward. The practitioner maintains pulling tension on the opponent's right arm and slides his right foot next to the inside of the opponent's right foot (if it isn't already situated there).

The practitioner slides his right hand under and around the right side of the opponent's neck in order to grab the back of his neck. Keep the fingers close together and the thumb on the back side of the neck. At this point in the technique, the chest is positioned close to the front of the opponent, facing the opponent's left, oblique, rear direction.

The practitioner throws the opponent forward by clutching the opponent's head tightly with his (i.e. the practitioner's) right arm and guiding the head toward the Tatame. He twists his upper torso in an approximately 180-degree counterclockwise direction, slides his left foot back, and goes down onto his left knee and the ball of his foot in order to generate power for this throw. The opponent is

Block to strike.

Aiki Sei Otoshi (grab wrist, pull arm and grip neck).

Aiki Sei Otoshi (twist and slide back).

Aiki Sei Otoshi (drop and throw the opponent).

Aiki Sei Otoshi (finish).

propelled over the practitioner's right knee into a Yoko Chugaeri (see Chapter 4). An opponent with no falling experience would probably fall forward, hit the Tatame and possibly injure his limbs in an effort to break his fall.

Block.

Aiki Sei Otoshi (grab wrist, pull arm and grip neck).

Strike.

Aiki Sei Otoshi (drop and throw the opponent).

Aiki Sei Otoshi: Performed at the Left Side of the Body

From a similar attack emanating from an opponent's left hand, the throw is performed in a manner similar to that described for the right side of the body. In this case, the initial retaliation to the opponent's attack is to evade to the inside of the opponent's strike using Migi Ude Ki Uke and to counter with a Hidari Gedan Oi Tate Tsuki (left lower-level vertical lunging fist strike) to the opponent's ribs. Subsequent to throwing the opponent, the practitioner quickly assumes a standing position and reassumes Hidari Hanmi Dachi (see Chapter 3) or follows with a wrist or arm-breaking technique (see Chapter 8).

Shomen-Uchi, Aiki Sei Otoshi: Shoulder Drop from a Vertical 'Head Cut' Samurai Sword Attack

Shomen-Uchi, Aiki Sei Otoshi is performed using two different methods: one from an evasion to the right side of the sword

Shomen Uchi, Aiki Sei Otoshi (grab wrist, pull arm and grip neck).

Shomen Uchi, Aiki Sei Otoshi (twist and slide back).

Shomen Uchi, Aiki Sei Otoshi (drop and throw the opponent).

Shomen Uchi, Aiki Sei Otoshi (opponent on the mat).

Shomen Uchi, Aiki Sei Otoshi (grab the hilt).

Shomen Uchi, Aiki Sei Otoshi (take the sword).

and the other from an evasion to the left side of the sword.

1. Using the evasion and striking technique to the right side of a Shomen-Uchi from Hidari Hanmi Dachi (see Chapter 3), perform the throwing technique in a manner similar to that described for Aiki Sei Otoshi. If the opponent, now lying on the Tatame, is still holding the sword with the hands correctly positioned apart (with the right hand gripping just below the hand guard and the left hand gripping the lower part of the hilt near the pommel), the practitioner uses his right hand to grab the exposed portion of the hilt between the opponent's grip, while simultaneously standing and pulling the sword up and out of the opponent's hand with a strong upward twist of his own wrist. The practitioner now lifts the hilt overhead into the upper-level guard position in preparation for the vertical 'down-cut'

that is employed as a finishing technique against the opponent on the Tatame.

2. Using the evasion and striking technique to the left side of a Shomen-Uchi from Hidari Hanmi Dachi (see Chapter 3), use the right hand to grab the opponent's right wrist and elevate the opponent's arm. Reposition the left foot slightly forward to the front, right, oblique direction in order to slide the left arm below the opponent's right arm and then up and around the back of the opponent's neck. Throw the opponent by taking an additional step forward using the right foot, cranking the opponent's head downward using the left arm, and dropping onto the left knee for power. Return to the standing position and grab the lower part of the sword's hilt using the left hand. Release the opponent's wrist and place the right, open hand flat onto the back of the blade in order to prepare for a 'supported cut' directed to the opponent's neck. The opponent will release the sword as this cut is performed because it is difficult to maintain a strong grip to the hilt in this awkward position, while lying on the Tatame.

Aiki Tai Otoshi: Body Drop

Aiki Tai Otoshi can be performed from the inside of a straight or roundhouse strike from an oppo-

Shomen Uchi, Aiki Sei Otoshi (position the hand on the opponent's neck).

Shomen Uchi, Aiki Sei Otoshi (slide forward).

Shomen Uchi, Aiki Sei Otoshi (drop and throw the opponent 1).

Shomen Uchi, Aiki Sei Otoshi (drop and throw the opponent 2).

Shomen Uchi, Aiki Sei Otoshi (grab the hilt).

Shomen Uchi, Aiki Sei Otoshi (take the sword).

Shomen Uchi, Aiki Sei Otoshi (place the hand onto the back of the sword).

Shomen Uchi, Aiki Sei Otoshi (Sasse Uchi).

Hidari Hanmi Dachi (against an opponent).

Aiki Tai Otoshi (block to strike).

Aiki Tai Otoshi (grab hand and twist).

nent's right or left hand. From an attack emanating from the opponent's right hand, evade to the right, forward, oblique direction using Hidari Ude Ki Uke and use the right hand to perform Migi Gedan Oi Tate Tsuki (right lower-level vertical lunging fist strike) to the opponent's ribs. Using painstaking care not to break contact between the left blocking arm and the opponent's right arm, slide the left hand up the arm and grab the opponent's right hand. (It makes no difference whether the opponent's fist is clenched or if the hand is open at this point… this should not impede the grab to his hand.) The practitioner twists the opponent's hand outward, away from himself (i.e. the practitioner) so the opponent's palm faces in an upward direction. This simple twist is achieved by bending the left hand back at the wrist in order to grab the opponent's hand from beneath and rotating it until the palm

turns downward, causing the opponent's palm to face in an upward direction.

Maintain twisting tension on the opponent's right arm in order to cause discomfort to the opponent's joints. Slide the right hand down the opponent's left arm in order to grab onto the topside of his left hand. Rotate the left arm down and up in a vertical, clockwise fashion until it's in the 9 o'clock position. The inside of the opponent's left elbow should now be positioned firmly against the bottom of his right elbow. The arms should cross creating an arm-locking, painful hold. The right arm of the practitioner is used to apply upward pressure beneath the opponent's right elbow, while, at the same time, the practitioner's left arm is used to pull the opponent's right arm down. Slide the right foot beyond and to the front of the opponent's right foot. Slide the left foot back in the rear direction and twist counter-

Aiki Tai Otoshi (slide hand to grab the opponent's hand).

Aiki Tai Otoshi (grab hand).

Aiki Tai Otoshi (rotate the opponent's arm).

Aiki Tai Otoshi (slide to the outside).

Aiki Tai Otoshi (twist into Kokutsu Dachi).

Aiki Tai Otoshi (draw the opponent's arms to throw 1).

Aiki Tai Otoshi (draw the opponent's arms to throw 2).

Aiki Tai Otoshi (throw finished).

Aiki Tai Otoshi (elbow break technique).

clockwise approximately 180 degrees to reposition into Migi Kokutsu Dachi (*see* Chapter 3). Simultaneous with the foot movement, throw the opponent by drawing his arms to his front direction and then downward at an oblique angle from the right to left side. During the throw, the practitioner's right, outstretched leg makes contact with the opponent's right knee, causing a trip or a necessity to jump into a Yoko Chugaeri (*see* Chapter 4). Subsequent to the throw, if necessary, select an *appropriate* finishing technique from the Katame Waza section of this book or simply slide back from the opponent and reassume Hidari Hanmi Dachi (*see* Chapter 3).

Hidari Hanmi Dachi (against an opponent).

Block.

Strike.

Aiki Tai Otoshi (grab hands and position them for the throw).

Aiki Tai Otoshi (slide into place and draw the arms forward).

Aiki Tai Otoshi Performed at the Left Side of the Body

From a similar attack emanating from an opponent's left hand, the throw is performed in a manner similar to that described for the right side of the body.

In this case, the initial retaliation to the opponent's attack is to evade to the inside of the opponent's strike using Migi Ude Ki Uke and to counter with a Hidari Gedan Oi Tate Tsuki (left lower-level vertical lunging fist strike) to the opponent's ribs.

Gyaku Age Uchi, Aiki Tai Otoshi (grab the hand).

Gyaku Age Uchi, Aiki Tai Otoshi (lift the arms).

Gyaku Age Uchi, Aiki Tai Otoshi: Reverse Rising Cut to Body Drop

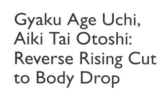

Against an opponent attacking with Gyaku Age Uchi using the Samurai sword, use the straight evasion to the rear from Hidari

Gyaku Age Uchi, Aiki Tai Otoshi (slide the foot outside).

Gyaku Age Uchi, Aiki Tai Otoshi (slide into place and draw the arms forward to throw 1).

Gyaku Age-Uchi, Aiki Tai Otoshi (slide into place and draw the arms forward to throw 2).

*Gyaku Age Uchi, Aiki Tai Otoshi
(grab the hilt).*

*Gyaku Age Uchi, Aiki Tai Otoshi
(adjust the grip).*

*Gyaku Age Uchi, Aiki Tai Otoshi
(take the sword).*

Hanmi Dachi (see Chapter 3). Do not reposition the (left) hand that was used to grab onto the opponent's right wrist during the strike to the ribs. Use the right hand to grab the topside of the opponent's hand from below. Without altering the opponent's grip or the sword's position, slide the right foot beyond and to the front of the opponent's right foot. Use both arms to draw the opponent forward and throw him down onto the Tatame by twisting approximately 180 degrees in a counterclockwise direction, repositioning into Migi Kokutsu Dachi.

Recover from the throwing technique by using the right hand to grab the exposed portion of the hilt between the opponent's hands. Slide back slightly and pull the sword up and out of the opponent's hand with a strong upward twist of the wrist in order to lift the sword overhead into Joden Kumai (upper-level sword guard). This will position the

practitioner for a finishing cut to the opponent's body that now lies on the Tatame.

Aiki Soto Tekubi Nage: Outer Wrist Throw

Aiki Soto Tekubi Nage is performed from the outside of a straight attack from an opponent's right or left hand. From an attack emanating from the opponent's right hand, evade to the left, forward, oblique direction using Migi Ude Ki Uke and follow by sliding the left foot forward one more step to strike the side of the opponents ribs using Hidari Gedan Oi Tate Tsuki (left lower-level vertical lunging fist strike).

Using the right hand, grab around the inside of the opponent's right hand with the thumb placed on

*Hidari Hanmi Dachi (against
an opponent).*

*Aiki Soto Tekubi Nage (evade,
block and strike).*

*Aiki Soto Tekubi Nage
(grab the hand).*

Aiki Soto Tekubi Nage (lift the arm).

Aiki Soto Tekubi Nage.

*Aiki Soto Tekubi Nage
(enter under arm).*

*Aiki Soto Tekubi Nage (apply
downward pressure).*

*Aiki Soto Tekubi Nage
(drop and throw).*

*Aiki Soto Tekubi Nage
(throw finished).*

the topside, and the middle and ring fingers gripping firmly on the underside of the hand just below the opponent's thumb. The practitioner slides the left foot back and cocks the opponent's hand by twisting the palm toward and then away from himself, in an ascending direction, in order to elevate the opponent's arm. Enter under the opponent's arm by sliding the body forward on the ball of the left foot. Twist the opponent's right hand over and apply downward pressure to the top of the hand with the thumb, causing much discomfort to his wrist. Turn clockwise 90-degrees on the ball of the left foot and slide the right foot back onto the knee and the ball of the foot to complete the throw.

Variation For additional support and power for the throwing technique, use two hands to complete the throw after entering under the opponent's arm. Rest the left, open palm on top of the right thumb (i.e. the practitioner's) and

orient it perpendicular to the right arm. Then proceed by twisting and pushing downward onto the hand in order to force the opponent onto the Tatame.

Aiki Soto Tekubi Nage (two handed version).

*Aiki Soto Tekubi Nage
(two-handed version).*

*Aiki Soto Tekubi Nage (twist
hand and push down).*

*Aiki Soto Tekubi Nage
(throw finished).*

Subsequent to either method, stand quickly and reassume Hidari Hanmi Dachi (see Chapter 3) or follow with a wrist- or arm-breaking technique.

Aiki Soto Tekubi Nage: Performed at the Left Side of the Body

From a similar attack emanating from an opponent's left hand, the throw is performed in a manner similar to that described for the right side of the body. In this case, the initial retaliation to the opponent's attack is to evade to the outside of the opponent's strike using Hidari Ude Ki Uke and to counter with a Migi Gedan Oi Tate Tsuki (right lower-level vertical lunging fist strike) to the opponent's ribs. Subsequent to throwing the opponent, stand quickly and reassume Hidari Hanmi Dachi or follow with a wrist- or arm-breaking technique (see Chapter 8).

Nuki Dashi, Soto Tekubi Nage: Outer Wrist Throw from Sword Draw

Soto Tekubi Nage is performed from a straight evasion to the rear against a Nuki-Dashi Age (rising sword draw) (see Chapter 3). After striking the opponent's ribs, the practitioner continues gripping the opponent's right wrist with his left hand. The practitioner then slides his right foot back to create just enough room to guide the opponent's sword down and then high up to the front, right side of his (i.e. the practitioner's) body. Enter under the opponent's arm by turning 90-degrees clockwise on the ball of the right foot. Use the right hand to grab the hilt of the sword just below the opponent's right hand. The practitioner then twists the hilt forward,

Aiki Soto Tekubi Nage (elbow break technique).

Evade and block.

Strike.

Aiki Soto Tekubi Nage (grab the hand).

Aiki Soto Tekubi Nage (grab).

Aiki Soto Tekubi Nage (slide forward, under the opponent's arm).

Aiki Soto Tekubi Nage (hand twist).

Aiki Soto Tekubi Nage (twist and slide back).

Aiki Soto Tekubi Nage (twist hand).

Aiki Soto Tekubi Nage (drop and throw).

Aiki Soto Tekubi Nage (throw finished).

Evade and strike.

Nuki Dashi, Soto Tekubi Nage (slide foot).

Nuki Dashi, Soto Tekubi Nage (move the sword carefully).

away from his body, and slides his left hand from the opponent's wrist onto the topside of the opponent's right hand. Use the left hand to pull downward on the opponent's hand causing discomfort to his wrist, off-balancing him to his rear. Pull the sword out of the opponent's grip using the right hand and throw him down to his rear using the left hand. Release the opponent's right hand. Slide the right hand up the hilt just below the hand guard and bring the sword up to Joden Kumai (upper-level guard position) to prepare for a finishing cut to the opponent who is lying on the Tatame.

Nuki Dashi, Soto Tekubi Nage (twist).

Nuki Dashi, Soto Tekubi Nage (enter under arm).

Nuki Dashi, Soto Tekubi Nage (lower arm).

Nuki Dashi, Soto Tekubi Nage (grab hilt).

Nuki Dashi, Soto Tekubi Nage (twist hilt and apply hand).

Nuki Dashi, Soto Tekubi Nage (push downward to throw).

Nuki Dashi, Soto Tekubi Nage (take sword).

Nuki Dashi, Soto Tekubi Nage (assume sword guard position).

Aiki Kote Gaeshi: Minor Wrist Overturn

Aiki Kote Gaeshi can be performed most efficiently from a straight or roundhouse attack directed toward the ribs, stomach or abdominal area of the body. From a straight attack emanating from the opponent's right hand, directed toward the ribs, perform Hidari Gedan Te Uke (left lower-level hand block) and retaliate with a right Reiken Uchi (back knuckle strike) to the opponent's face.

The practitioner grabs the opponent's right hand using the left hand and rotates it about 45-degrees clockwise, positioning the thumb onto the topside of the opponent's hand and the middle and ring fingers on the bottom side of the opponent's hand. Use the thumb to press tightly into the fleshy area located between the tendons of the opponent's fingers. Position the right palm partially on top of the left thumb and grip the area around the topside of the opponent's fingers. Maintaining a strong two-handed grip, slide the right foot forward toward the opponent and strike the left side of the opponent's chin with the elbow. Throw the opponent forward by twisting his hand counterclockwise at the wrist

Hidari Hanmi Dachi (against an opponent).

Gedan Te Uke (lower block).

Gedan Te Uke.

Migi Reiken Uchi (back knuckle strike).

and cranking it up and down in an arc-like fashion. The latter is performed by the practitioner sliding his left foot back in tandem with a counterclockwise twist on the right foot, finishing in Jigohontai Dachi (neutral stance) (see Chapter 3). Follow with Kataha Gatame (single wing lock) (see Chapter 8) or release the opponent's hand and reassume Hidari Hanmi Dachi (see Chapter 3).

Aiki Kote Gaeshi (grab hand).

Aiki Kote Gaeshi.

Aiki Kote Gaeshi (grab hand).

Aiki Kote Gaeshi.

Aiki Kote Gaeshi.

Aiki Kote Gaeshi (slide forward and elbow strike).

Aiki Kote Gaeshi (twist body and twist wrist).

Aiki Kote Gaeshi (throw).

Aiki Kote Gaeshi (throw finished).

Aiki Kote Gaeshi (wrist breaking technique).

Aiki Kote Gaeshi: Performed at the Left Side of the Body

Aiki Kote Gaeshi is performed at the left side of the body in a manner that is almost identical to the method used at the right side. The footwork that is used during the block to the opponent's straight attack (aimed at the ribs) positions the body for a follow-up strike using a front, rather than reverse, posture. This eliminates the need for a strike to the chin and a step forward, with the left foot, toward the opponent. Complete the throw in the same manner as described for the right side of the body.

Block.

Strike.

Aiki Kote Gaeshi (grab hand).

Aiki Kote Gaeshi (twist wrist and crank arm).

Aiki Kote Gaeshi (throw finished).

Aiki Kote Gaeshi (control arm).

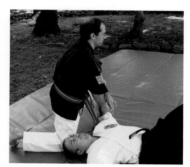

Aiki Kote Gaeshi (drop onto knee and wrist break).

Nuki Dashi, Aiki Kote Gaeshi: Minor Wrist Overturn Against a Sword Draw

Use the pre-emptive, straight invasion from Hidari Hanmi Dachi against an opponent's attempt to draw his sword (see Chapter 3). After striking at the opponent's chin, use the left hand to keep his wrist secured against the front of his body. Use the right hand to grab the hilt behind the opponent's grip, slide back using the right foot and withdraw the sword from the scabbard. This will easily break

Invade, block the sword and strike.

Nuki Dashi, Aiki Kote Gaeshi (grab hilt).

Nuki Dashi, Aiki Kote Gaeshi (take sword).

the opponent's grip of the sword's handle, injuring his thumb to the degree to which the sword is held tightly by the opponent.

Slide the left hand onto the opponent's right hand, grabbing the topside with the thumb and the bottom-side with the remaining fingers gripping from below. Twist the opponent's wrist counter-clockwise and guide his arm up and over to the left in an arc-like fashion, causing great discomfort to the opponent's joints. Maintain pressure on the opponent's wrist in order to keep him from moving and choke-up on the hilt by sliding your right hand just beneath the hand-guard. Place the blade against the right side of the opponent's neck, slide forward with the right foot and move the blade toward the opponent's rear as if to cut the opponent. The practitioner throws the opponent forward by guiding the opponent's right arm back to the right in

Nuki Dashi, Aiki Kote Gaeshi (direct sword to side).

Nuki Dashi, Aiki Kote Gaeshi (twist hand).

Nuki Dashi, Aiki Kote Gaeshi (sword to neck).

Nuki Dashi, Aiki Kote Gaeshi (slide foot and cut).

Nuki Dashi, Aiki Kote Gaeshi (tap leg and cock hand).

Nuki Dashi, Aiki Kote Gaeshi (drop and crank arm).

Nuki Dashi, Aiki Kote Gaeshi (throw and cut).

Nuki Dashi, Aiki Kote Gaeshi (throw finished).

Nuki Dashi, Aiki Kote Gaeshi (assume sword guard position).

an arc-like fashion. This is the means by which he 'loads' the throw. The thrower then taps his right leg with his left foot, twists the opponent's wrist counterclockwise and guides the opponent's arm up and over toward the front of the opponent. The sword would be used to help guide the opponent forward and to make a deeper cut to the side of the opponent's neck. To prevent the sword's blade from colliding with the opponent's legs on the somersault break-fall, slide the sword along the side of the opponent's neck and direct it to the rear as the opponent flips over.

After the opponent falls onto the Tatame, let go of the opponent's right hand and slide the right foot forward toward the opponent. Bring the sword overhead into Joden Kumai (upper-level guard) to prepare for a finishing cut to the opponent who is lying on the Tatame.

Aiki Morote Seio Nage: Two-Handed Shoulder Throw

Aiki Morote Seio Nage is performed from the outside of a straight attack from an opponent's right or left hand. From an attack emanating from the opponent's right hand, evade to the left, forward, oblique direction using Migi Ude Ki Uke. Follow by sliding the left foot forward one more step in order to strike the side of the opponent's ribs using Hidari Gedan Oi Tate Tsuki (left lower-level vertical lunging fist strike).

Using the right hand, grab around the right side of the opponent's right hand with the thumb placed on the topside, and the middle and ring fingers gripping firmly on the underside of the hand just below the opponent's thumb, similar to Aiki Soto Tekubi Nage. Use the left hand to reach below the opponent's right arm (across the front of the opponent's body) and grab the opponent's left hand, clasping it palm to palm. The practitioner slides his left foot back and cocks both of the opponent's hands back, making sure to twist his right palm toward his body. He then reverses the direction of the opponent's hands and guides them away from himself in an ascending direction in order to lift the opponent's arms high. Enter under the opponent's arms by sliding the body forward on the ball of the left foot, assuming Jigohontai Dachi (neutral stance) (see Chapter 3), positioning the back of the body next to and to the front of the opponent's body. The practitioner guides the opponent's arms over to the right side of the practitioner's head and sets the opponent's right elbow firmly onto the practitioner's right shoulder. The opponent's left elbow is now positioned sideways against the right side of practitioner's neck, using the neck as a fulcrum. The practitioner deepens his knees in order to position his hips just below the level of the opponent's waist. He then throws the opponent over his right shoulder by pulling the opponent's hands downward in order to put pressure on both of the opponent's elbows. At the same time, the practitioner delivers a hard thrust upward using his hips.

Hidari Hanmi Dachi (against an opponent).

Block.

Strike.

Aiki Morote Seio Nage (grab hand).

Aiki Morote Seio Nage (reach below arm).

Aiki Morote Seio Nage (grab hand).

Aiki Morote Seio Nage (slide back and cock arms).

Aiki Morote Seio Nage (grips).

Aiki Morote Seio Nage (arms up).

Aiki Morote Seio Nage (grips).

Aiki Morote Seio Nage (arms across).

Aiki Morote Seio Nage (arms extended forward).

Aiki Morote Seio Nage (using hips and arms to throw).

Aiki Morote Seio Nage (throw).

Aiki Morote Seio Nage (throw finished).

Subsequent to throwing the opponent, slide the right foot back and assume Hidari Hanmi Dachi (see Chapter 3).

Aiki Morote Seio Nage: Performed at the Left Side of the Body

From a similar attack emanating from an opponent's left hand, the throw is performed in a manner similar to that described for the right side of the body. The initial retaliation to the opponent's attack is to evade to the outside of the opponent's strike using Hidari Ude Ki Uke and to counter with a Migi Gedan Oi Tate Tsuki (right lower-level vertical lunging fist strike) to the opponent's ribs (see Chapter 3).

Elbow and grab.

Shomen-Uchi, Aiki Morote Seio Nage: Two-Handed Shoulder Throw from a Vertical 'Head Cut' Samurai Sword Attack

Using the evasion and striking technique to the left side of a Shomen-Uchi from Hidari Hanmi Dachi (see Chapter 3), grab both hands and perform the throw in a manner similar to that which was described to the outside of straight attack with the opponent's right hand. Recover by using the right hand to grab the exposed portion of the hilt between the opponent's hands, if the opponent is still holding the hilt with two hands after the fall. Slide back slightly and pull the sword up and out of the opponent's hand

Shomen Uchi, Aiki Morote Seio Nage (grab hand).

Shomen Uchi, Aiki Morote Seio Nage (slide back and cock arms).

Shomen Uchi, Aiki Morote Seio Nage (slide forward and raise arms).

Shomen Uchi, Aiki Morote Seio Nage (grips).

Shomen Uchi, Aiki Morote Seio Nage (arms across).

Shomen Uchi, Aiki Morote Seio Nage (grips).

Shomen Uchi, Aiki Morote Seio Nage (arms forward and throw).

Shomen Uchi, Aiki Morote Seio Nage (throw finished).

Shomen Uchi, Aiki Morote Seio Nage (grab hilt).

Shomen Uchi, Aiki Morote Seio Nage (assume sword guard position).

with a strong, upward twist of the wrist in order to lift the sword overhead into Joden Kumai (upper-level guard). This will position the practitioner for a finishing cut to the opponent's body that now lies on the Tatame.

Exercise caution to avoid directing the blade's tip into the Tatame as the opponent is thrown over the shoulder. Use this throw against an opponent of similar or lesser height to diminsh the chance of this occurrence.

Aiki Ura Shiho Nage: Circular Four Winds Throw

Aiki Ura Shiho Nage can be performed from the inside of a straight or roundhouse strike from an opponent's right or left hand. From an attack emanating from the opponent's right hand, evade to the right, forward, oblique direction using Hidari Ude Ki Uke and use the right hand to perform Migi Gedan

Oi Tate Tsuki (right lower-level vertical lunging fist strike) to the opponent's ribs. Use the left hand to grab the opponent's right hand, palm facing palm, and guide it in a vertical, counterclockwise direction to the 6 o'clock position in front of the body. With the top of his left hand supported by the palm of his right hand, the practitioner creates a firm, two-handed grip to the opponent. Using both hands, continue to circle the opponent's hand upward in the same counterclockwise fashion toward the 12 o'clock position. Slide the left foot forward slightly and guide the opponent's arm overhead. Twist the body approximately 360-degrees clockwise on the left foot and slide the right foot around to the front of the body to assume Migi Zenkutsu Dachi (see Chapter 3). Bend the opponent's hand back and lower his arm by exerting pressure on his wrist in order to off-balance the opponent to the rear direction. Hold the opponent's hand at about the level of the opponent's shoulder and pin the opponent's arm using the practitioner's right forearm held tightly against the arm. This will keep the opponent from twisting to escape from the hold.

Slide the right foot back to the rear and begin to twist the wrist counterclockwise. Continue to twist the opponent's wrist and crank the arm downward, while spinning 180-degrees on the right foot. Slide the left foot around to the rear and descend onto the knee and the ball of the foot.

Be aware that this technique can easily injure an opponent's wrist and shoulders. An opponent must yield to this technique by, in essence, jumping into a high somersault over the wrist-locking technique to escape the pin, landing into a perfect side break-fall.

Hidari Hanmi Dachi (against an opponent).

Block and strike.

Aiki Ura Shiho Nage (grab and guide downward).

Aiki Ura Shiho Nage (both hands hold).

Aiki Ura Shiho Nage (grip).

Aiki Ura Shiho Nage (guide hand upward).

Aiki Ura Shiho Nage (grip).

Aiki Ura Shiho Nage (grip after twist).

Aiki Ura Shiho Nage (bend and pin arm).

Aiki Ura Shiho Nage (off-balance).

Aiki Ura Shiho Nage: Performed at the Left Side of the Body

From a similar attack emanating from an opponent's left hand, the throw is performed in a manner similar to the way it was described at the right side of the body. In this case, the initial retaliation to the opponent's attack is to evade to the inside of the opponent's strike using Migi Ude Ki Uke and to counter with a Hidari Gedan Oi Tate Tsuki (left lower-level vertical lunging fist strike) to the opponent's ribs. Subsequent to throwing the opponent, stand quickly and reassume Hidari Hanmi Dachi.

As an aside, the title 'Shiho Nage' was chosen for this technique because the throw can easily be used to throw an

Aiki Ura Shiho Nage (slide back).

Aiki Ura Shiho Nage (twist and slide back).

Aiki Ura Shiho Nage (slide back and drop to throw).

Aiki Ura Shiho Nage (throw finished).

Hidari Hanmi Dachi (against an opponent).

Block.

Strike.

Aiki Ura Shiho Nage (grab hand).

Aiki Ura Shiho Nage (guide hand up).

Aiki Ura Shiho Nage (bend and pin arm).

opponent to all of the four basic directions of the compass.

Shomen-Uchi, Aiki Ura Shiho Nage: Circular Four Winds Throw from a Vertical 'Head Cut' Samurai Sword Attack

Use the pre-emptive straight invasion against a Shomen-Uchi from Hidari Hanmi Dachi and block the opponent's arms before the blade begins to descend downward toward the head (see Chapter 3). Using the left hand, grab the hilt between the opponent's grip on the sword's handle and slide the left foot to the outside of the opponent's right foot. Pull the hilt back to the left, front, oblique direction, thereby off-balancing the opponent in that direction. Using his right hand, the practitioner grabs the opponent's right hand from below and (with his left hand) 'peels' the hilt out of the opponent's hand, bringing the blade safely to the left side of the practitioner's body. He then positions his right elbow against the opponent's ribs to maintain pressure to the left, front, oblique direction in order keep the opponent from escaping the wrist and shoulder lock.

The practitioner throws the opponent forward by using the right hand, without the support of the

Invasive block.

Shomen Uchi, Aiki Ura Shiho Nage (grab hilt).

Shomen Uchi, Aiki Ura Shiho Nage (off-balance).

Shomen Uchi, Aiki Ura Shiho Nage (take sword).

Shomen Uchi, Aiki Ura Shiho Nage (twist).

Shomen Uchi, Aiki Ura Shiho Nage (drop and throw).

Shomen Uchi, Aiki Ura Shiho Nage (throw finished).

Shomen Uchi, Aiki Ura Shiho Nage (release hand and grip sword).

Shomen Uchi, Aiki Ura Shiho Nage (assume sword-guard position).

left hand, to crank the opponent's arm outward and forward in a fashion similar to the method described in Aiki Shiho Nage. The practitioner simultaneously slides his left foot back on the ball of the foot, twisting 180-degrees counterclockwise on the right foot and dropping onto the left knee and the ball of the foot. The blade should be positioned safely to the rear, out of the way of the opponent, who somersaults over the practitioner's right knee and into the left side break-falling position on the Tatame. Immediately subsequent to the throw, position the sword to the front of the body and use the right hand to grab the hilt just below the left hand. Release the grip with the left hand and slide the right hand up the hilt, just below the hand guard. Stand straight up and bring the blade overhead into Joden Kumai (upper-level guard) in order to prepare for a finishing cut to the opponent who is now lying on the Tatame.

Aiki Ashi Kaiten Nage: Leg Rotary Throw

Aiki Ashi Kaiten Nage can be performed from the inside of a straight or roundhouse strike from an opponent's right or left hand. From an attack emanating from the opponent's right hand, evade to the right, forward, oblique direction using Hidari Ude Ki Uke and use the right hand to perform Migi Gedan Oi Tate Tsuki (right lower-level vertical lunging fist strike) to the opponent's ribs.

Slide the right foot slightly to the front, right, oblique direction and place the right, open hand onto the lower portion of the opponent's left quadriceps, just above the knee. The practitioner simultaneously places his left, open hand onto the back of the opponent's neck, with the fingers pointing away from himself. Throw the opponent forward

Hidari Hanmi Dachi (against an opponent).

Block and strike.

Aiki Ashi Kaiten Nage (grabbing leg and neck).

Aiki Ashi Kaiten Nage (twist, drop and throw).

Aiki Ashi Kaiten Nage (throw finished).

by guiding the opponent's head down and lifting his left leg up in a high circle with a small circumference, tumbling the opponent's body forward and upside-down into a somersault. In tandem with the hand movements, in order to generate power for this throw, slide the left foot back on the ball of the foot, twist 180-degrees counterclockwise on the right foot, and drop onto the left knee and the ball of the left foot. Stand and position into Hidari Hanmi Dachi (see Chapter 3).

Aiki Ashi Kaiten Nage: Performed at the Left Side of the Body

From a similar attack emanating from an opponent's left hand, the throw is performed in a manner similar to the way it was described for the right side

Hidari Hanmi Dachi (against an opponent).

Block.

Strike.

Aiki Ashi Kaiten Nage (grabbing leg and neck).

Aiki Ashi Kaiten Nage.

Aiki Ashi Kaiten Nage (twist and throw 1).

Aiki Ashi Kaiten Nage (drop and throw 2).

Aiki Ashi Kaiten Nage (throw finished).

of the body. In this case, the initial retaliation to the opponent's attack is to evade to the inside of the opponent's strike using Migi Ude Ki Uke and to counter with a Hidari Gedan Oi Tate Tsuki (left lower-level vertical lunging fist strike) to the opponent's ribs. Subsequent to throwing the opponent, stand quickly and reassume Hidari Hanmi Dachi.

Shomen-Uchi, Aiki Ashi Kaiten Nage: Leg Rotary Throw from a Vertical 'Head Cut' Samurai Sword Attack

Using the evasion and striking technique to the right side of a Shomen-Uchi from Hidari Hanmi Dachi (see Chapter 3), perform the throwing technique at the right side of the body similar to the manner which

was described in Aiki Ashi Kaiten Nage. Subsequent to the throw, stand straight up and slide the right foot back to reposition into Hidari Hanmi Dachi.

Evasion and elbow strike.

Shomen Uchi, Aiki Ashi Kaiten Nage
(reaching).

Shomen Uchi, Aiki Ashi Kaiten Nage
(grabbing leg and neck).

Shomen Uchi, Aiki Ashi Kaiten Nage
(twist, drop and throw).

Shomen Uchi, Aiki Ashi Kaiten Nage
(throw finished).

Migi Hanmi Dachi.

Hidari Hanmi Dachi.

Evade and block.

Strike.

Similar to any technique in which an opponent might be falling with a sword, he must employ extreme caution not to direct the sword toward himself or into the Tatame, and must direct the sword to the side. The best falling method to use for this throw is Iai Mae Zempo Kaiten (front rotary roll) with the sword unsheathed. This can be done with one or two hands gripping the hilt.

Aiki Ude Kaiten Nage: Arm Rotary Throw

Aiki Ude Kaiten Nage is performed from the outside of a straight attack from an opponent's right or left hand. From an attack emanating from the opponent's right hand, evade to the left, forward, oblique direction using Migi Ude Ki Uke and follow by sliding the left foot forward one more step to strike the side of the opponent's ribs using Hidari Gedan Oi Tate Tsuki (left lower-level vertical lunging fist strike).

'Load' the opponent's right arm by using the palms of both hands to slap the opponent's arm downward and backward. The force to accomplish the latter is generated by the practitioner as he taps his right leg with his left foot and drops into Jigohontai Dachi (see Chapter 3). As the opponent begins to lean forward, place the right, open hand

Aiki Ude Kaiten Nage (tap leg and lift arms).

Aiki Ude Kaiten Nage (slap arms downward).

*Aiki Ude Kaiten Nage (grab hand and
position hand on neck).*

onto the back of the opponent's neck and slide the left hand up the underside of the opponent's right arm in order to grab the topside of the opponent's right hand from beneath. Push downward on the opponent's neck and bend the opponent's right hand, directing it upward (causing discomfort to the opponent's wrist) and forcing him to bend to an approximately 90-degree angle relative to the Tatame.

The practitioner now taps his left leg with his right foot, twists 90-degrees to the right and throws the opponent by using his (i.e. the practitioner's)

Aiki Ude Kaiten Nage (tap leg).

*Aiki Ude Kaiten Nage (drop and
throw).*

*Aiki Ude Kaiten Nage (throw
finished).*

hands to rotate the opponent's head and right arm in a tight, vertical, clockwise circle. Drop onto the left knee and the ball of the left foot. Stand up and slide the right foot back to reposition into Hidari Hanmi Dachi (see Chapter 3).

Note: the opponent's right arm is guided up and to the right, in a circular fashion, from approximately the 9 o'clock position to the 3 o'clock position, while his head is guided downward and to the left, from approximately the 3 o'clock position to the 9 o'clock position. The opponent falls using Yoko Chugaeri (see Chapter 4).

Aiki Ude Kaiten Nage: Performed at the Left Side of the Body

From a similar attack emanating from an opponent's left hand, the throw is performed in a manner similar to that described for the right side of the body. In this case, the initial retaliation to the opponent's attack is to evade to the outside of the opponent's strike using Hidari Ude Ki Uke and to counter with a Migi Gedan Oi Tate Tsuki (right lower-level vertical lunging fist strike) to the opponent's ribs. Finish the throw with a 90-degree twist to the left and drop onto the right knee and the ball of the right foot. Subsequent to the throw, stand and slide back, recovering directly into Hidari Hanmi Dachi.

This throw is *not* performed against a Samurai sword attack.

Hidari Hanmi Dachi.

Evade and block.

Strike.

Aiki Ude Kaiten Nage (tap leg).

Aiki Ude Kaiten Nage (slap arms downward).

Aiki Ude Kaiten Nage (grab hand and position hand on neck).

Aiki Ude Kaiten Nage (tap leg).

Aiki Ude Kaiten Nage (throw 1).

Aiki Ude Kaiten Nage (throw 2).

Aiki Ude Kaiten Nage (throw finished).

CHAPTER 7

JU-JUTSU NAGE WAZA: HIP THROWS AND SWEEPS

Ippon Seio Nage: One-Arm Shoulder Throw

Ippon Seio Nage can be performed from the inside of a straight or roundhouse strike coming from an opponent's right or left hand. From an attack emanating from the opponent's right hand, evade to the right, forward, oblique direction using Hidari Ude Ki Uke and use the right hand to perform Migi Gedan Oi Tate Tsuki (right lower-level vertical lunging fist strike) to the opponent's ribs.

Using the left hand, the practitioner grabs the opponent's right wrist or sleeve just above the wrist. He then pulls the opponent's arm forward in order to off-balance him toward a forward direction. The practitioner slides his right hand under and around the opponent's right arm in order to grab the Gi (uniform) in the area of the right bicep. Maintaining forward tension on the opponent's right arm, the practitioner twists counterclockwise on his right foot and slides his left foot back so that the feet are aligned side by side. The back of the

Hidari Hanmi Dachi (against an opponent).

Block and strike.

Ippon Seio Nage (grab and pull).

Ippon Seio Nage (slide arm under).

Ippon Seio Nage (grab).

Ippon Seio Nage (twist).

Ippon Seio Nage (bend knees).

Ippon Seio Nage (bend back and pull arm).

Ippon Seio Nage (lift).

Ippon Seio Nage (throw).

Ippon Seio Nage (throw finished).

Hidari Hanmi Dachi.

practitioner's body is now positioned against the front of the opponent's body.

With his knees bent deeply enough, so that his hips are positioned below the level of the opponent's waist, the thrower's right hip is shifted outward, situating it slightly beyond the right side of the opponent's body. He draws the opponent's right arm further and bends forward at the waist, thereby causing the opponent to fall over and onto his back. Using great force, the practitioner propels the opponent over his hips by twisting his (i.e. the thrower's) upper torso counterclockwise and straightening his legs at the knees and ankles.

After the opponent falls onto the Tatame, the practitioner holds onto the opponent's right arm with both hands, pulls it upward and positions his (i.e. the practitioner's) legs for Ude Hishigi Juji

Gatame (cross arm lock) (see Chapter 8). As an alternative to groundwork, the thrower merely lets go of the opponent and slides his right foot back and reassumes Hidari Hanmi Dachi.

Ippon Seio Nage: Performed at the Left Side of the Body

From a similar attack emanating from an opponent's left hand, the throw is performed in a manner similar to that described for the right side of the body. In this case, the initial retaliation to the opponent's attack is to evade to the inside of the opponent's strike using Migi Ude Ki Uke and to counter with a Hidari Gedan Oi Tate Tsuki (left lower-level vertical lunging fist strike) to the opponent's ribs. Follow with groundwork or simply shift back into Hidari Hanmi Dachi.

Hidari Hanmi Dachi (against an opponent).

Block.

Strike.

Ippon Seio Nage (pull arm).

Ippon Seio Nage (slide arm under).

Ippon Seio Nage (grab).

Ippon Seio Nage (twist).

Ippon Seio Nage (bend knees).

Koshi Guruma: Hip Wheel

Koshi Guruma can be performed from the inside of a straight or roundhouse strike coming from an opponent's right or left hand. From an attack emanating from the opponent's right hand, evade to the right, forward, oblique direction using Hidari Ude Ki Uke and use the right hand to perform Migi Gedan Oi Tate Tsuki (right lower-level vertical lunging fist strike) to the opponent's ribs.

Using his left hand, the practitioner grabs the opponent's right wrist or sleeve just above the wrist. He then pulls the opponent's arm forward to off-balance the opponent in a forward direction and slides his right hand around the back of the opponent's neck to grab the uniform on top of the opponent's right shoulder. Maintaining forward tension on the opponent's right arm, the practitioner

Ippon Seio Nage (bend back and pull arm).

Ippon Seio Nage (lift and throw 1).

Ippon Seio Nage (lock knees and spring upward 2).

Ippon Seio Nage (throw finished).

Hidari Hanmi Dachi (against an opponent).

Block and strike.

Koshi Guruma (grab).

Koshi Guruma (pull arm).

Koshi Guruma (grab).

Koshi Guruma (twist and align feet).

Koshi Guruma (bend knees).

Koshi Guruma (bend back and pull arm).

Koshi Guruma (lift).

Koshi Guruma (twist and throw).

Koshi Guruma (drop).

Koshi Guruma (land on opponent).

Groundwork.

twists counterclockwise on his right foot and slides his left foot back to align his feet side by side. The back of the practitioner's body is now positioned against the front of the opponent's body.

With his knees bent deeply enough so that his hips are positioned below the level of the opponent's waist, the practitioner's right hip is shifted outward, situating it slightly beyond the right side of the opponent's body. He draws the opponent's right arm further and bends forward at the waist, causing the opponent to fall over and onto his back. Using great force, the practitioner propels the opponent over his hips by twisting his (i.e. the practitioner's) upper torso counterclockwise and straightening his legs at the knees and ankles. The practitioner falls

with the opponent, so the side of his body collides with the opponent's ribcage upon impact with the Tatame. The arms and body will be perfectly positioned on the opponent to use Kesa Gatame (scarf hold) (see Chapter 8) as a follow-up technique.

Note: falling onto an opponent during any throwing technique can cause serious damage to the opponent's body. In this particular case, the opponent's ribs can be injured easily. During training, decrease this risk by lightly falling onto your partner just subsequent to the throw.

As an alternative to groundwork, throw the opponent and remain standing. Release the opponent's arm and slide the right foot back to reassume Hidari Hanmi Dachi.

Koshi Guruma (throw finished).

Hidari Hanmi Dachi.

Koshi Guruma: Performed at the Left Side of the Body

From a similar attack emanating from an opponent's left hand, the throw is performed in a manner similar to that described for the right side of the body. In this case, the initial retaliation to the opponent's attack is to evade to the inside of the opponent's strike using Migi Ude Ki Uke and to counter with a Hidari Gedan Oi Tate Tsuki (left lower-level vertical lunging fist strike) to the opponent's ribs. Upon conclusion of the throw, fall onto the opponent (to follow-up with groundwork) or remain standing, let go of the opponent's left arm and shift back into Hidari Hanmi Dachi.

Hidari Hanmi Dachi (against an opponent).

Block.

Strike.

Koshi Guruma (grab arm and pull).

Koshi Guruma (slide arm around neck).

Koshi Guruma (grab uniform).

Koshi Guruma (different angle).

Koshi Guruma (twist).

Koshi Guruma (bend knees).

Koshi Guruma (pull and lift).

Koshi Guruma (throw).

Koshi Guruma (fall).

Groundwork.

Hidari Hanmi Dachi.

O Soto Gari: Major Outer Clip

O Soto Gari can be performed from the inside of a straight or roundhouse strike coming from an opponent's right or left hand. From an attack emanating from the opponent's right hand, evade to the right, forward, oblique direction using Ude Ki Uke and use the right elbow to perform Yoko Empi Uchi (side elbow strike) to hit the left side of the opponent's chin, causing the opponent to off-balance to the left, oblique direction.

Using his left hand, the practitioner grabs around the upper portion of the opponent's right arm and secures the arm tightly against the left side of his (i.e. the practitioner's) body, with the opponent's wrist and/or hand resting under the armpit. Grab the opponent's closest lapel deeply, beyond the right side of the opponent's neck. Slide the left foot out to the front, left, oblique direction, positioning it slightly to the outside of the opponent's right foot. The practitioner off-balances the opponent to this direction by pulling his right arm downward, and pushing down on his shoulder and chest, using the right hand that is gripping the Gi lapel. The practitioner achieves leverage for this manipulation by bending his own back forward slightly and twisting his upper torso counterclockwise.

Note: exercise caution not to lean the opponent back to an angle exceeding 45 degrees lest he fall before there is an opportunity to sweep the leg.

Hidari Hanmi Dachi (against an opponent).

Block and strike.

O Soto Gari (grab).

O Soto Gari (pin arm).

O Soto Gari (grab uniform and off-balance).

O Soto Gari (lift leg).

O Soto Gari (sweep leg 1).

O Soto Gari (sweep leg 2).

O Soto Gari (hold on and recover leg).

O Soto Gari (drop for groundwork).

Without allowing the opponent to straighten his back, the practitioner raises his right leg so that his thigh is parallel to the Tatame, points his toes downward, and sweeps the opponent's right leg. In one powerful 'kick', the 'sweeping leg' begins at the 9 o'clock position, collides with the opponent's leg at approximately the 5 o'clock position, and continues all the way around to the 3 o'clock position, ending

O Soto Gari (release opponent).

Hidari Hanmi Dachi.

with the leg extended out to the rear direction. The calf is used to perform this sweep and makes contact with the back of the opponent's knee, forcing the opponent to fall backward.

Subsequent to the throw, the practitioner's right arm is positioned on the opponent's neck to easily perform Ude Osae Jime (arm press choke) (see Chapter 8) by dropping onto the right knee. As an alternative, recover from the sweep by standing (straight) and then shifting back to resituate into Hidari Hanmi Dachi.

O Soto Gari: Performed at the Left Side of the Body

From a similar attack emanating from an opponent's left hand, the throw is performed in a manner similar to that described for the right side of the body. In this case, the initial retaliation to the opponent's

Hidari Hanmi Dachi (against an opponent).

Block.

Strike.

O Soto Gari (grab).

O Soto Gari (pin arm).

O Soto Gari (grab uniform and off-balance).

O Soto Gari (lift leg).

O Soto Gari (sweep leg).

O Soto Gari (throw finished).

O Soto Gari (drop for groundwork).

attack is to evade to the inside of the opponent's strike using Migi Ude Ki Uke and to counter with a left Yoko Empi Uchi (side elbow strike) directed to the right side of the opponent's chin. After throwing the opponent, the practitioner either stands (straight) and slides his right foot back to assume Hidari Hanmi Dachi (see Chapter 3) or follows-up using groundwork in a manner similar to that described for the right side of the body.

Uki Goshi: Minor Hip Throw

Uki Goshi can be performed from the inside of a straight or roundhouse strike coming from

Hidari Hanmi Dachi (against an opponent).

Block and strike.

an opponent's right or left hand. From an attack emanating from the opponent's right hand, evade to the right, forward, oblique direction using Hidari Ude Ki Uke and use the right hand to perform Migi Gedan Oi Tate Tsuki (right lower-level vertical lunging fist strike) to the opponent's ribs.

Using his left hand, the practitioner grabs the opponent's right wrist or sleeve just above the wrist. He pulls the arm forward to off-balance the opponent to a forward direction and slides his right hand around the opponent's back to position it opened, on the far side of the opponent's waist. The practitioner slides his left foot back behind his right foot to assume a deep Kosa Dachi (cross stance)

(see Chapter 3) and positions the right side of his hip below the opponent's waist, at the centre of the body. The opponent is thrown over the practitioner's hip by drawing the opponent's arm forward as the practitioner twists his own upper torso counterclockwise, 'bumping' or lifting the opponent up and quickly dropping him off the right side of the hip. Release the opponent and slide the right foot back to assume Hidari Hanmi Dachi. As an alternative, drop onto the opponent during the throw and adjust the arms to assume Kesa Gatame (scarf hold) (see Chapter 8).

Note: the position of the hips for this throw is dissimilar to the other hip throws presented in this

Uki Goshi (grab).

Uki Goshi (pull arm and reach around waist).

Uki Goshi (slide foot back).

Uki Goshi (twist, pull arm and bump with hip).

Uki Goshi (throw).

Uki Goshi (throw finished).

Hidari Hanmi Dachi.

Uki Goshi (drop).

Groundwork.

book because the thrower's hip does not extend beyond the side of the opponent's body. The hip is positioned to the centre of the opponent's body, in essence, 'bumping' one of the opponent's hips as opposed to directing the whole width of the body over the hip.

Uki Goshi: Performed at the Left Side of the Body

From a similar attack emanating from an opponent's left hand, the throw is performed in a manner similar to that described for the right side of the body. In this case, the initial retaliation to the opponent's

Hidari Hanmi Dachi (against an opponent).

Block.

Strike.

Uki Goshi (pull arm and off-balance).

Uki Goshi (twist into cross stance).

Uki Goshi (throw).

Uki Goshi (drop).

Groundwork.

Hidari Hanmi Dachi.

attack is to evade to the inside of the opponent's strike using Migi Ude Ki Uke and to counter with a Hidari Gedan Oi Tate Tsuki (left lower-level vertical lunging fist strike) to the opponent's ribs. Upon conclusion of the throw, fall onto the opponent to follow up with groundwork or remain standing by releasing the opponent as he falls. Shift back and assume Hidari Hanmi Dachi.

Tomoe Nage: Stomach Throw

Tomoe Nage can be performed from the inside of a straight or roundhouse strike coming from an opponent's right or left hand. From an attack emanating from the opponent's right hand, evade to the right, forward, oblique direction using Hidari Ude Ki Uke and use the right fist to perform Ue Tsuki (uppercut) to strike the bottom of the opponent's jaw, causing the opponent to rise slightly onto the balls of the feet.

Using the left hand, the practitioner grabs around the upper portion of the opponent's right arm and secures the arm tightly against the left side of his (i.e. the practitioner's) body, with the opponent's wrist and/or hand resting under the practitioner's armpit, similar to O Soto Gari (see Chapter 7). Grab the opponent's closest lapel deeply, beyond the right side of the opponent's neck. Slide the left foot forward to a position just behind the right foot and, using both hands, lift the opponent onto the balls of his feet. Without allowing the opponent to ground himself by returning flat onto the soles of his feet, the practitioner lifts his own right leg and places the ball of his right foot onto the front of the opponent's body, pressing on the edge of the ribcage in the area of the stomach. Throw the opponent by drawing him close to the body, dropping onto the buttocks and 'kicking' by extending the right leg straight out, thereby launching the opponent upside down to his front, left, oblique direction. Quickly return to the standing position, turn around and assume Hidari Hanmi Dachi (see Chapter 3).

Hidari Hanmi Dachi (against an opponent).

Block and strike.

Tomoe Nage (grab and pin arm).

Tomoe Nage (grab lapel).

Tomoe Nage (slide foot and lift).

Tomoe Nage (position foot at stomach).

Tomoe Nage.

Tomoe Nage (drop and pull).

Tomoe Nage (thrust using foot).

Tomoe Nage (release opponent).

Tomoe Nage (hold on and pull yourself over).

Groundwork.

To follow with groundwork, use both hands to pull downward to hoist your body over and on top of the opponent as he falls to the rear. Land with the buttocks resting on top of the opponent's stomach and the legs straddling the opponent's body, your knees and feet positioned on the Tatame. Use Gyaku Juji Jime (reverse cross choke) (see Chapter 8) after freeing the left-handed grip to the opponent's uniform in the area of his arm.

Tomoe Nage: Performed at the Left Side of the Body

From a comparable attack emanating from an opponent's left hand, the throw is performed in a manner similar to that described for the right side of the body. In this case, the initial retaliation to the opponent's attack is to evade to the inside of the opponent's strike using Migi Ude Ki Uke and to counter with a left Ue Tsuki (upper-cut) to the bottom of the opponent's jaw.

Hidari Hanmi Dachi (against an opponent).

Block.

Strike.

Tomoe Nage (grab and pin arm).

Tomoe Nage (grab lapel).

Tomoe Nage (slide foot and lift).

Tomoe Nage (position foot at stomach).

Tomoe Nage (drop and pull).

Tomoe Nage (thrust using foot).

Tomoe Nage (release opponent).

Groundwork.

Note: always direct the opponent's body in an oblique direction as he falls forward. Do not direct an opponent straight overhead, as he might fall on top of your body if the throw doesn't work as planned.

Harai Goshi: Sweeping Loin Throw

Harai Goshi can be performed from the inside of a straight or roundhouse strike coming from an opponent's right or left hand. From an attack emanating from the opponent's right hand, evade to the right, forward, oblique direction using Hidari Ude Ki

Uke and use the right hand to perform Migi Gedan Oi Tate Tsuki (right lower-level vertical lunging fist strike) to the opponent's ribs.

Using the left hand, the practitioner grabs the opponent's right wrist or sleeve just above the wrist, pulling the arm forward in an ascending fashion, lifting the opponent's body weight onto the tips of his toes, thereby off-balancing the opponent to a forward direction. Slide the right hand around the opponent's back to position it open, on the far side of his waist. The practitioner aligns the back of his body against the front of the opponent's body by twisting in a counterclockwise direction and sliding his left foot back just behind his right foot to assume

Hidari Hanmi Dachi.

Block and strike.

Harai Goshi (grab and pull arm).

Harai Goshi (slide into cross stance and reach around the opponent's back).

Harai Goshi (pull arm and sweep leg to throw 1).

Harai Goshi (throw 2).

Hidari Hanmi Dachi.

Harai Goshi (hold onto opponent).

Kosa Dachi (cross stance) (see Chapter 3). Pull the opponent's right arm further forward, drop flat onto the sole of the left foot, and use the right leg to sweep the opponent's right leg just above the knee. Keep the right leg as straight as possible during the sweep and do not hook the opponent's leg. The right hamstrings make contact with the opponent's right leg and the upper torso twists counterclockwise to throw the opponent forward over the right hip. Release the opponent and recover by swinging the right leg back next to the left leg, straightening the body vertically. Slide the right foot back and assume Hidari Hanmi Dachi (see Chapter 3). As an alternative, hold onto the opponent's right arm, thereby preventing him from falling far forward. Drop onto the right knee and perform Kata Gatame (shoulder hold) (see Chapter 8).

Note: the momentum for this throw begins immediately following the strike to the opponent's ribs and the moves to follow blend together into one, non-stop flowing technique. Similar to any hip throw discussed in this book, forward tension to the opponent's 'throwing arm', preventing the opponent from re-rooting himself, is maintained throughout the throwing technique. This throw was designed to be used against an opponent of similar or greater height when compared to the practitioner.

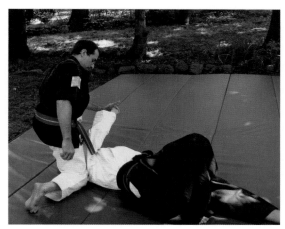

Harai Goshi (drop onto knee).

Groundwork.

Harai Goshi: Performed at the Left Side of the Body

From a comparable attack emanating from an opponent's left hand, the throw is performed in a manner similar to that described for the right side of the body. In this case, the initial retaliation to the opponent's attack is to evade to the inside of the opponent's strike using Migi Ude Ki Uke and to counter with a Hidari Gedan Oi Tate Tsuki (left lower-level vertical lunging fist strike) to the opponent's ribs.

At the conclusion of the throw, hold onto the opponent's arm to follow with groundwork or completely release the opponent as he falls. Swing the left leg back to straighten the body vertically and follow by sliding the right foot back to assume Hidari Hanmi Dachi.

Hidari Hanmi Dachi.

Block.

Strike.

Harai Goshi (grab arm and reach around the opponent's back).

Harai Goshi (slide into cross stance).

Harai Goshi (sweep leg and throw 1).

Harai Goshi (throw 2).

Harai Goshi (hold onto opponent).

Harai Goshi (drop onto the knee and control arm).

Groundwork.

Hidari Hanmi Dachi.

Uchi Mata: Inner Thigh Throw

Uchi Mata can be performed from the inside of a straight or roundhouse strike coming from an opponent's right or left hand. From an attack emanating from the opponent's right hand, evade to the right, forward, oblique direction using Hidari Ude Ki Uke and use the right hand to perform Migi Gedan Oi Tate Tsuki (right lower-level vertical lunging fist strike) to the opponent's ribs.

Using the left hand, the practitioner grabs the opponent's right wrist or sleeve just above the wrist, pulling the arm forward to off-balance the opponent to a forward direction, shifting the majority of the opponent's body weight onto his right leg.

Hidari Hanmi Dachi (against an opponent).

Block and strike.

Uchi Mata (grab sleeve and off-balance).

Uchi Mata (grab lapel).

Uchi Mata (slide back).

Uchi Mata (sweep leg and pull forward to throw 1).

Using the right hand, grab the opponent's closest lapel high up, beyond the left side of the neck. Twist counterclockwise and slide the left foot behind and in line with the right foot

Do not position the feet into a tight Kosa Dachi (cross stance), as required in some of the other throwing techniques. This position will situate the left foot too far to the opponent's front, right side, thereby hindering a sweep to his left leg.

Use both hands to pull the opponent in a forward and then descending direction and sweep the inside of the opponent's left leg upward. Make contact with the opponent's inner thigh, just above the knee, using the back of the right knee. Release the opponent and recover by swinging your right

Uchi Mata (throw 2).

Uchi Mata (release opponent).

Hidari Hanmi Dachi.

Uchi Mata (hold onto opponent).

Uchi Mata (drop onto knee).

Groundwork.

leg back, next to your left leg, straightening your body vertically. Slide the right foot back and assume Hidari Hanmi Dachi. As an alternative, hold onto the opponent's arm and uniform lapel, thereby preventing him from falling far forward. Drop onto the right knee, release your grip on the opponent's right hand, and perform Ude Osae Jime (arm press choke) (see Chapter 8).

Note: similar to Harai Goshi, momentum for this throw begins immediately following the strike to the opponent's ribs, and the moves to follow blend together into one, non-stop flowing technique. Forward tension to the opponent's 'throwing arm' is maintained throughout the throwing technique, preventing the opponent from re-rooting himself.

This throw was designed to be used against an opponent of equal or lesser height, as compared to the practitioner. The thrower must be tall enough to sweep the opponent's leg to an angle greater than 90-degrees relative to the Tatame in order to cause the opponent to flip forward involuntarily.

Uchi Mata: Performed at the Left Side of the Body

From a comparable attack emanating from an opponent's left hand, the throw is performed in a manner similar to that described for the right side of the body. In this case, the initial retaliation to the opponent's attack is to evade to the inside of the opponent's strike using Migi Ude Ki Uke and

Hidari Hanmi Dachi.

Block.

to counter with a Hidari Gedan Oi Tate Tsuki (left lower-level vertical lunging fist strike) to the opponent's ribs.

At the conclusion of the throw, hold onto the opponent's uniform to follow-up with groundwork or completely release the opponent as he falls. Swing the left leg back to straighten the body vertically and follow by sliding the right foot back to assume Hidari Hanmi Dachi.

Strike.

Uchi Mata (grab arm and pull).

Uchi Mata (grab lapel).

Uchi Mata (grips).

Uchi Mata (slide back).

Uchi Mata (pull opponent and sweep to throw 1).

Uchi Mata (throw 2).

Uchi Mata (throw 3).

Uchi Mata (hold onto opponent).

Uchi Mata (drop onto knee).

Groundwork.

Uchi Mata (release opponent).

Hane Goshi: Spring Hip Throw

Hane Goshi can be performed from the inside of a straight or roundhouse strike coming from an opponent's right or left hand. From an attack emanating from the opponent's right hand, evade to the right, forward, oblique direction using Hidari Ude Ki Uke and use the right hand to perform Migi Gedan Oi Tate Tsuki (right lower-level vertical lunging fist strike) to the opponent's ribs.

Using the left hand, the practitioner grabs the opponent's right wrist or sleeve just above the wrist, pulling his arm forward in an ascending fashion, lifting the opponent's body weight onto the tips of the toes and off-balancing the opponent to a forward direction. Slide the right hand around the opponent's back to position it open, on the far side of the waist. Align the right side of the body against the front of the opponent's body by twisting in a counterclockwise direction and sliding the left foot back, just behind the right foot, to assume Kosa Dachi (cross stance) (see Chapter 3). Pull the opponent's right arm further forward, drop flat onto the sole of the left foot and lift the right knee so the thigh is perfectly horizontal, positioned in line with the opponent's hips. The lower portion of the right leg, from the knee to the toes, rests vertically against the inside of the opponent's right leg. The right foot is bent at the ankles, with the toes directed downward so that the topside of the foot rests against the inside of the opponent's leg. Throw the opponent over the top of the practitioner's right leg and hip by using the left hand to pull the opponent forward… upward and outward… in a diagonal direction. Using the right hand, the practitioner positions his arm around the opponent's waist to steer him over the side of his right hip and thigh. This is accomplished by bending slightly forward and twisting the upper torso counterclockwise.

Release the opponent and step back with the right foot to assume Hidari Hanmi Dachi. As an alternative manoeuvre, hold onto the opponent's right arm, thereby preventing the opponent from falling far forward. Drop onto the right knee and perform Kata Gatame (shoulder hold) (see Chapter 8).

Hidari Hanmi Dachi (against an opponent).

Block to strike.

Hane Goshi (grab and pull arm).

Hane Goshi (slide into cross stance and reach around opponent' s back).

Similar to Harai Goshi, momentum, non-stop flow and forward tension to the opponent's 'throwing arm' are pivotal elements to making this technique work. While I have found this throw to be effective against most opponents, it is most appropriately employed against an opponent of similar height or taller than the practitioner.

Hane Goshi (lift leg and pull opponent).

Hane Goshi (throw over leg).

Hidari Hanmi Dachi.

Hane Goshi (hold onto opponent).

Hane Goshi (drop onto knee).

Groundwork.

Hane Goshi: Performed at the Left Side of the Body

From a comparable attack emanating from an opponent's left hand, the throw is performed in a manner similar to that described for the right side of the body. In this case, the initial retaliation to the opponent's attack is to evade to the inside of the opponent's strike using Migi Ude Ki Uke and to counter with a Hidari Gedan Oi Tate Tsuki (left lower-level vertical lunging fist strike) to the opponent's ribs. Upon conclusion of the throw, release the opponent, stand on two feet and then step back with the right foot to assume Hidari Hanmi Dachi. As an alternative, hold onto the opponent's left arm, preventing him from falling far forward, and follow with groundwork.

Hidari Hanmi Dachi (against an opponent).

Block.

Strike.

Hane Goshi (grab arm).

Hane Goshi (pull arm and slide into cross stance).

Hane Goshi (lift leg).

Hane Goshi (throw).

Hidari Hanmi Dachi.

Hane Goshi (hold onto the opponent).

Hane Goshi (drop onto the knee).

Groundwork.

Tsuri Komi Goshi: Lift Pull Hip Throw

Tsuri Komi Goshi can be performed from the inside of a straight or roundhouse strike coming from an opponent's right or left hand. From an attack emanating from the opponent's right hand, evade to the right, forward, oblique direction using Hidari Ude Ki Uke and use the right hand to perform Migi Gedan Oi Tate Tsuki (right lower-level vertical lunging fist strike) to the opponent's ribs.

Using the left hand, the practitioner grabs the opponent's right wrist or sleeve just above the wrist, pulling the arm forward to off-balance the opponent to a forward direction. Using the right hand, grab the opponent's closest lapel high up, beyond the left side of the neck. Maintaining forward tension on the opponent's right arm, twist counterclockwise on the right foot and slide the left foot back to align the feet side by side, positioning the back of the body flush against the front of the opponent's body.

Hidari Hanmi Dachi (against an opponent).

Block and strike.

Tsuri Komi Goshi (grab arm).

Tsuri Komi Goshi (grab lapel).

Tsuri Komi Goshi (twist, align feet and bend knees).

Tsuri Komi Goshi (pull opponent onto the back).

Tsuri Komi Goshi (throw 1).

Use the right-handed grip to the opponent's lapel to lift him onto the balls of the feet and bend deeply at the knees, positioning the hips below the level of the opponent's waist. Shift the right hip outward, situating it slightly beyond the right side of the opponent's body. The practitioner draws the opponent's right arm further forward and bends his own back forward at the waist, thereby causing the opponent to fall onto his (i.e. the practitioner's) back. Using great force, propel the opponent over your hips by twisting the upper torso counterclockwise and straightening the legs at the knees and ankles.

Tsuri Komi Goshi (throw 2).

Tsuri Komi Goshi (hold onto the opponent).

Tsuri Komi Goshi (grab hand and straddle the opponent).

Tsuri Komi Goshi (drop onto the knee and elbow the opponent).

Groundwork.

As the opponent falls toward the Tatame, slide the right hand up the opponent's right sleeve in order to grab his right hand. Turn to the left in order to drop onto the front of the opponent's body to perform Ude Garami (arm entanglement) (see Chapter 8). As an alternative, after the throw, release the grip to the opponent's uniform and slide the right foot back to assume Hidari Hanmi Dachi.

Hidari Hanmi Dachi.

Tsuri Komi Goshi: Performed at the Left Side of the Body

From a comparable attack emanating from an opponent's left hand, the throw is performed in a manner similar to that described for the right side of the body. In this case, the initial retaliation to the opponent's attack is to evade to the inside of the opponent's strike using Migi Ude Ki Uke and to counter with a Hidari Gedan Oi Tate Tsuki (left lower-level vertical lunging fist strike) to the opponent's ribs. Subsequent to throwing the opponent, follow up with groundwork or simply release the opponent and shift back into Hidari Hanmi Dachi.

Hidari Hanmi Dachi (against an opponent).

Block.

Strike.

Tsuri Komi Goshi (grab and pull arm).

Tsuri Komi Goshi (grab lapel).

Tsuri Komi Goshi (twist into position and bend knees).

Tsuri Komi Goshi (pull opponent onto the back to throw 1).

Tsuri Komi Goshi (spring hips upward to throw 2).

Tsuri Komi Goshi (throw 3).

Tsuri Komi Goshi (grab the hand and straddle the opponent).

Tsuri Komi Goshi (drop onto the knee and elbow the opponent).

Groundwork.

Hidari Hanmi Dachi.

Sode Tsuri Komi Goshi: Sleeve Lift Pull Hip Throw

While Sode Tsuri Komi Goshi is performed in the same manner as Tsuri Komi Goshi, the grip to the opponent differs slightly. For a throw at the right side of the body, the right hand is used to grab the cuff at the end of the opponent's left sleeve (as opposed to grabbing the lapel). For a throw at the left side of the body, the left hand is used to grab the cuff at the end of the opponent's right sleeve. In each case, the opponent's arm is held vertically by lifting and pressing the side of the forearm against the inside of the opponent's forearm.

Hidari Hanmi Dachi (against an opponent).

Block and strike.

Sode Tsuri Komi Goshi (grab sleeve and pull downward).

Sode Tsuri Komi Goshi (grab cuff).

Sode Tsuri Komi Goshi (pull arm and insert forearm against opponent's other arm).

Sode Tsuri Komi Goshi (twist to align the body and bend knees).

Sode Tsuri Komi Goshi (pull arms and lift to throw 1).

Sode Tsuri Komi Goshi (thrust hips upward to throw 2).

Sode Tsuri Komi Goshi (release opponent).

Hidari Hanmi Dachi
(against an opponent).

Block.

Strike.

Sode Tsuri Komi Goshi (grab arm).

Sode Tsuri Komi Goshi (grab cuff).

Sode Tsuri Komi Goshi (pull arm and insert forearm against opponent's other arm).

Sode Tsuri Komi Goshi (pull arm and lift to throw 1).

Sode Tsuri Komi Goshi (twist to align the body and bend knees).

Sode Tsuri Komi Goshi (thrust hips upward to throw 2).

Sode Tsuri Komi Goshi (throw 3).

Sode Tsuri Komi Goshi (release opponent).

Hidari Hanmi Dachi.

Follow with groundwork (see Chapter 8) by dropping onto the opponent during or after he has fallen onto the Tatame. As an alternative to groundwork, release the opponent and slide back to resituate into Hidari Hanmi Dachi.

Sode Tsuri Komi Goshi (drop onto the knee for groundwork).

Sode Tsuri Komi Goshi (from a right-side throw, hold onto the opponent's arm).

Sode Tsuri Komi Goshi (drop onto the knee for groundwork).

Sode Tsuri Komi Goshi (from a left-side throw, hold onto the opponent's arm).

CHAPTER 8

KATAME WAZA: GROUNDWORK 'HOLDING' TECHNIQUES

The idea of subduing an opponent and bringing him to the ground, looks and sounds exciting. In the United States today, the public appears to be extremely interested in ground fighting, and the media, to an unprecedented degree, is fuelling this curiosity by offering regular programming that includes relevant content. Reflect, for a moment, upon the life of a Samurai during the Sengoku Period, a period in Japanese history characterized by anarchy, continual fighting and unstable leadership. Now contemplate what it might be like to have just turned the 'wrong' corner, walking alone on a deserted city street when, to your surprise, four thugs approach you with intentions of doing you harm. Would you attempt to subdue your opponents to the ground? If you have this goal in mind, you may find many obstacles that might prevent you from doing this effectively: you risk the chance of falling onto something hard, bumpy or sharp, such as a concrete or asphalt surface, rocks or even glass. In addition, while you are focusing your energies on subduing one opponent at a time, you run the risk of being subdued by your other opponents. Let's not forget the axiom of the Jujutsu component of Aiki-Jujutsu, which is to make use of *the most efficient method of defence* to overcome your opponents.

Groundwork does, indeed, have its deserved place in the canon of Aiki-Jujutsu. The appropriate context for its application is, however, for it to be executed in a safe, efficient and effective manner. There is a time and a place for everything. In real combat, use the following groundwork techniques only if you (1) have been pulled down by your opponent during a throw, (2) have inadvertently lost balance and have fallen onto your opponent, or (3) have been taken by surprise, having been already reclining or sitting on the ground.

Kesa Gatame: Scarf Hold

Kesa Gatame is easily performed subsequent to Koshi Guruma (see Chapter 7), because the hands and body are practically in position for the first part of the hold. Fall onto the opponent's ribcage as the opponent falls over the right side of your body and onto the Tatame. Keep the right arm positioned around the back of the opponent's neck, with the right hand grasping the opponent's uniform above the far shoulder. Use the left hand to grab around the upper portion of the opponent's right arm to secure his arm tightly against the left side of your body, with the opponent's wrist and/or hand resting under your armpit. The side of the practitioner's legs are positioned against the Tatame, as if he were running and caught on camera, mid-stride. The right leg is bent and high above the left leg, with the edge of both feet pressing downward into the mat. The left leg is positioned below using the same configuration. Both feet are bent upward at the ankles, and the toes are directed upward as well. The practitioner turns his head to the left, away from the opponent, and presses the back of his head into the side of the opponent's head or face, preventing him from twisting toward the practitioner's body. Squeeze the opponent's neck and right arm tightly and lean all of the body weight downward, into the side of the opponent, causing his breathing to become laboured.

Kesa Gatame (from Koshi Guruma).

Kesa Gatame (falling onto opponent).

Kesa Gatame (arm around neck).

Kesa Gatame (secure arm at side).

Kesa Gatame (head against opponent's head).

Hadaka Jime (open hand).

Hadaka Jime (clasp hands).

Hadaka Jime (exert pressure).

Hadaka Jime.

To finish the opponent:

1. Hadaka Jime (Naked Choke). Release the hold on the opponent's right arm and slide your left hand over to your right hand in order to clasp it, palm to palm. Exert upward pressure on the side of the opponent's neck, using the right forearm, and lean the right shoulder downward, onto the opponent's jaw or neck. This manoeuvre causes extreme pain to the jaw, head or neck area and should prompt the opponent to submit.

2. Hiji Ori (Elbow Break). Keep pressure on the opponent's neck, using the right shoulder and the right forearm, sandwiching the neck like a vice grip. Open the left hand, slide it down the opponent's right arm, and grab the opponent's wrist. Pull forward to straighten the opponent's arm and turn it so the back of the elbow can be positioned to lie on top of the inside of the right thigh. Exert downward pressure onto the opponent's elbow by using the left hand to press his arm down. Perform this manoeuvre slowly, giving your opponent the opportunity to submit, lest otherwise his arm be badly injured.

Hiji Ori (from Kesa Gatame).

Hiji Ori (release grip and slide down arm).

Hiji Ori (grab wrist).

Hiji Ori (position elbow on thigh and exert pressure).

Kesa Gatame is performed at the left side of the body in a manner similar to that described for the right side of the body.

BOTTOM LEFT: *Kesa Gatame (fall onto opponent).*

BOTTOM RIGHT: *Kesa Gatame (arm around neck).*

Kesa Gatame (secure arm at side).

Hadaka Jime (open hand).

Hadaka Jime (clasp hands and exert pressure).

Hiji Ori (from Kesa Gatame).

Hiji Ori (release grip and slide down arm).

Hiji Ori (grab wrist).

Hiji Ori (position elbow on thigh and exert pressure).

Kata Gatame: Shoulder Hold

From Harai Goshi (see Chapter 7) performed at the right side of the body, use the left hand to hold onto the opponent's right arm as he falls onto the Tatame. Turn your body to an orientation perpendicular to the opponent, who is lying on the Tatame. With the practitioner now positioned at the right side of the opponent's body, he drops onto his right knee and the ball of his foot.

Slide the left hand onto the topside of the opponent's hand in order to grip it. Position the opponent's right arm tightly around the front of his neck

Kata Gatame (hold onto the opponent).

Kata Gatame (guide arm forward positioning the opponent on his side).

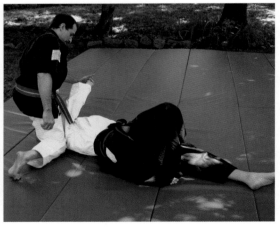

Kata Gatame (drop onto knee).

Kata Gatame (wrap arm around the neck and slide foot out).

Kata Gatame (slide forearm to the back of the neck).

Kata Gatame (grab wrist 1).

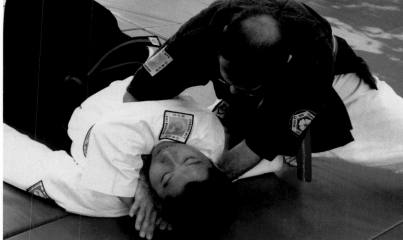

Kata Gatame (grab wrist 2).

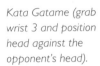

Kata Gatame (grab wrist 3 and position head against the opponent's head).

Kata Gatame (exert pressure).

or chin, and slide your left foot straight out to the rear, straightening your leg at the knee, positioning your foot flat on the mat, in line with the opponent's right shoulder. Slide your left forearm below the back of the opponent's neck without letting go of the opponent's right hand. Using the right hand, grab the opponent's right wrist, situating the inside of your forearm against the left side of the opponent's neck.

Position the right side of the head firmly against the right side of the opponent's head or face. Squeeze the opponent's head between your right forearm and the right side of your head. Pressure should be exerted gradually in order to allow the opponent time to submit, or he might be 'choked-out'.

Kata Gatame is performed at the left side of the body in a manner similar to that described for the right side of the body.

Kata Gatame (hold onto the opponent).

Kata Gatame (guide opponent onto his side and drop onto the knee).

Kata Gatame (wrap arm around neck).

Kata Gatame (slide foot out and position other knee against the opponent).

Kata Gatame (grab wrist).

Kata Gatame (exert pressure).

Ude Osae Jime: Arm Press Choke

Immediately following O Soto Gari (see Chapter 7), drop onto the right knee and continue the right hand grip to the uniform lapel. Twist the right arm to position the bone on the outer part of the forearm onto the front of the opponent's neck. Release the grip to the opponent's right arm, and place the left, open hand onto the inside of the forearm, in the area of the elbow. Use the whole body to apply downward pressure onto the opponent's neck by keeping your back erect and your left elbow as straight as possible. Apply gradual pressure so that the opponent can submit as opposed to risking injury to his neck.

Ude Osae Jime is performed at the left side of the body in a manner symmetrical to the way it was described for the right side of the body.

Ude Osae Jime (hold onto the opponent).

ABOVE: *Ude Osae Jime (drop onto the knee and position forearm against the neck).*

LEFT: *Ude Osae Jime (position hand onto forearm).*

Ude Osae Jime (exert pressure).

Gyaku Juji Jime: Reverse Cross Choke

Using Tomoe Nage to throw the opponent over the right side of your body, use both hands to pull downward to hoist your body over and on top of the opponent as he falls to the rear. Land with the buttocks resting on top of the opponent's stomach, with the legs straddling the opponent's body, the knees and balls of the feet situated on the Tatame. Squeeze the opponent between your thighs in order to limit his movement sideways. Let your right hand remain positioned on the opponent's right lapel. Release the left-handed grip to the opponent's sleeve and reach above your right arm to grab his left lapel by the side of the neck. The palm of your hand is directed away from the opponent's neck. Twist the outside of your forearms toward the opponent (similar to Ude Osae Jime) and pull the opponent's lapels so they dig into the sides of his neck. Bend forward, so that your chest leans against your arms, thereby causing downward pressure to the front of the opponent's neck. Rest your head against and to the left side of the opponent's head in order to prevent it from being grabbed.

Ude Osae Jime (hold onto the opponent).

Ude Osae Jime (drop onto the knee and position forearm against the neck).

Ude Osae Jime (position hand onto forearm and exert pressure).

Gyaku Juji Jime (hold onto the opponent and hoist yourself over and onto him).

Gyaku Juji Jime (straddling opponent).

Gyaku Juji Jime (grab other lapel).

Gyaku Juji Jime (twist arms and pull lapels).

Gyaku Juji Jime (bend forward onto arms).

Gyaku Juji Jime (position head against the opponent's head).

Gyaku Juji Jime (interweave legs).

Gyaku Juji Jime (attempt to straighten legs).

As a variation, intertwine your legs by sliding them under, to the inside of the opponent's legs, and then up, hooking the feet around the topside of the opponent's legs. Hold this position and forcefully attempt to straighten your legs at the knees. This will cause great discomfort to the opponent's legs when executed simultaneously with the reverse cross choke to the neck.

Gyaku Juji Jime is performed from a throw at the left side of the body in a manner similar to that described for a throw at the right side of the body.

Gyaku Juji Jime (hold onto the opponent and hoist yourself over and onto him).

Gyaku Juji Jime (straddling opponent).

Gyaku Juji Jime (reach over arm to grab lapel).

Gyaku Juji Jime (twist arms and pull lapels).

Gyaku Juji Jime (bend forward onto arms).

Gyaku Juji Jime (position head against the opponent's head).

Gyaku Juji Jime (interweave legs).

Gyaku Juji Jime (attempt to straighten legs).

Kataha Gatame: Single Wing Lock

Subsequent to throwing an opponent at the right side of the body with Aiki Kote Gaeshi (see Chapter 6), there would be no need for an adjustment of the two-handed grip to the opponent's right hand to use this wrist-locking technique. Just drop onto your left knee and the ball of the foot and press down on top of opponent's hand to position the opponent's forearm vertically, with his elbow rest-ing on the Tatame. Slide your right foot over to position the inside of the foot against the right side of the opponent's elbow in order to keep it from moving out of place. Straighten your back and arms at the elbows. Gradually apply pressure to the opponent's wrist by using the entire weight of the body to push downward onto the top of his hand. Release the pressure immediately after your training partner submits so you do not injure his wrist.

Kataha Gatame (hold onto the opponent).

Kataha Gatame (drop onto knee and straighten opponent's arm).

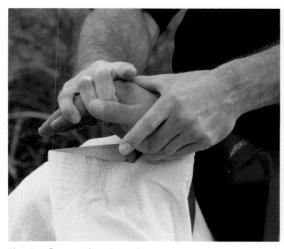

Kataha Gatame (hand grips).

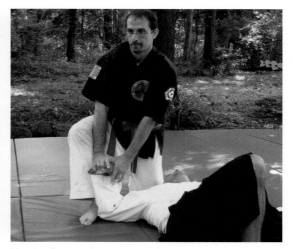

Kataha Gatame (exert pressure).

Kataha Gatame (hold onto the opponent).

BELOW: Kataha Gatame (straighten opponent's arm).

Kataha Gatame is performed using an opponent's left hand in a manner similar to that described using an opponent's right hand.

Kataha Gatame (drop onto knee and exert pressure).

Ude Gatame: Arm-Lock

Ude Gatame has three different variations: a standing method, a kneeling method and a method that is used against an opponent who, after falling, attempts to pull the thrower to the Tatame.

1. Standing Method. After throwing an opponent at the right side of the body using Aiki Tai Otoshi (*see* Chapter 6), maintain the grip to the opponent's right hand. Draw the opponent's arm to the left in order to straighten the arm at the elbow. Slide your right foot forward into Zenkutsu Dachi (forward stance) (*see* Chapter 3) and set the back of the opponent's elbow just below the kneecap. Apply gradual pressure to the elbow by pulling the opponent's arm slowly back toward the body, using the right leg as a fulcrum. Release the pressure to the elbow following submission by the opponent.

2. Kneeling Method. After performing Sode Tsuri Komi Goshi (*see* Chapter 7) to an opponent at the right side of the body, remain standing and slide your right hand up the opponent's right arm in order to grab his wrist. Guide his arm outward to the right in order to straighten the opponent's elbow. Drop onto the left knee and the ball of your foot and use your left thumb to apply pressure to the opponent's throat, thereby preventing him from moving. Similar to the standing method, place the back of his elbow against your leg, just below the kneecap, using the right leg as a fulcrum. Do not release pressure to the opponent's throat as you apply

Ude Gatame, standing method (hold hand after throw).

Ude Gatame, standing method (apply pressure to elbow).

pressure to the elbow, lest the opponent stand and escape from the technique.

3. Counter to a Pull Down Attempt. After performing Ippon Seio Nage (see Chapter 7) to an opponent at the right side of the body, the oppo-

nent reaches up to grab the uniform using his left, free hand with the intention to pull you down to the Tatame. Release grips to the opponent and place both of your palms, one hand positioned on top of the other, on the back of the opponent's left elbow.

Ude Gatame, kneeling method (after throw, slide hand to grab wrist).

Ude Gatame, kneeling method (drop onto knee and thumb to neck).

Ude Gatame, kneeling method (close-up).

Ude Gatame, kneeling method (position elbow against leg and apply pressure).

Slide your left foot straight back to the rear direction and press on the opponent's elbow, twisting the opponent onto the right side of his body. Direct downward pressure onto the opponent's elbow, and, to complete the technique, drop to your left knee and the ball of your foot so the opponent is pinned with his chest against the Tatame. Apply pressure to the elbow until the opponent submits.

In all three variations, Ude Gatame is performed in a similar manner at both sides of the body.

Ude Gatame, counter to pull down attempt (opponent grabs uniform).

Ude Gatame, counter to pull down attempt (position both hands on elbow).

Ude Gatame, counter to pull down attempt (slide back).

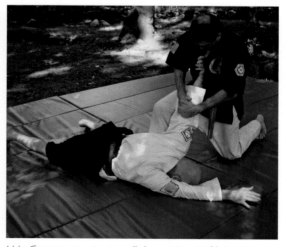

Ude Gatame, counter to pull down attempt (drop onto knee and apply pressure).

Ude Gatame, standing method (hold onto opponent after throw).

Ude Gatame, standing method (grab wrist, position elbow on leg and exert pressure).

Ude Gatame, kneeling method (hold onto opponent).

Ude Gatame, kneeling method (grab wrist and pull to straighten the arm).

Ude Gatame, kneeling method (drop onto knee and apply pressure to neck).

Ude Gatame, kneeling method (pull arm to back to exert pressure).

Ude Gatame, counter to pull down attempt (hold onto opponent).

Ude Gatame, counter to pull down attempt (opponent grabs uniform).

Ude Gatame, counter to pull down attempt (position both hands on elbow).

Ude Gatame, counter to pull down attempt (slide back).

Ude Gatame, counter to pull down attempt (drop onto knee and apply pressure).

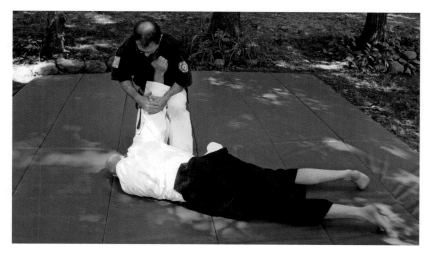

Ude Garami (hold onto opponent and release right hand grip).

BELOW: Ude Garami (turn to straddle the opponent).

Ude Garami (drop onto the knee and elbow opponent).

Ude Garami: Arm Entanglement

After throwing an opponent using Tsuri Komi Goshi (see Chapter 7) at the right side of the body, remain standing and release the right-handed grip to the opponent's lapel. Slide your right hand up the opponent's right sleeve to grab onto the topside of his hand. Turn counterclockwise in order to orient your body in such a way that it is similar to the orientation of the opponent's body as it lies on the Tatame. Use your right foot to step over the body in order to straddle him. Drop onto your right knee and gently elbow the opponent to the jaw, using your right arm. Do not release the grip to the opponent's right hand during the strike.

Drop onto your left knee and squeeze the opponent tightly between your thighs. Lean forward and direct pressure onto the opponent's right wrist by bending his hand downward. Rest the side of the opponent's arm onto the Tatame and intertwine your left arm with the opponent's right arm. Accomplish this by sliding your left hand below the opponent's triceps and then up and around to the topside of the opponent's right hand. Release the grip with your right hand and direct your right elbow against the side of the opponent's head, thereby causing discomfort to the opponent. Follow-up by quickly grabbing onto the topside of the opponent's right hand with your left hand and applying pressure to the wrist by bending the hand

Ude Garami (drop to both knees, straddle and squeeze the opponent).

Ude Garami (lean forward).

Ude Garami (slide hand under the opponent's arm).

Ude Garami (apply pressure to the head using the elbow).

Ude Garami (position the head against the opponent's head and apply pressure to the wrist).

Ude Garami (interweave legs 1).

Ude Garami (interweave legs 2).

Ude Garami (attempt to straighten the legs).

Ude Garami (hold hand, turn and straddle opponent).

ABOVE: Ude Garami (drop onto the knee and elbow opponent).

ABOVE: Ude Garami (rest opponent's elbow onto the mat).

Ude Garami (drop onto the knee).

Ude Garami (interweave arm with opponent's arm 1).

RIGHT: Ude Garami (interweave arm with opponent's arm 2).

LEFT: Ude Garami (grab wrist and apply pressure to head using elbow).

downward and leaning your left shoulder forward against the opponent's right triceps. Position your head next to and to the left of the opponent's head and gradually increase pressure to the opponent's wrist. Be sure to hold the opponent tightly between your thighs throughout the technique.

As an alternative for the legs, similar to Gyaku Juji Jime (see *above*), intertwine the legs by sliding them under, to the inside of the opponent's legs, and then up, hooking your feet around the topside of the opponent's legs. Hold this position and forcefully attempt to straighten your legs at the knees. This manoeuvre, along with the wrist-locking technique to the opponent's arm, will cause great discomfort to the opponent's legs. Ude Garami is performed using the opponent's left arm in a manner similar to that described using the opponent's right arm.

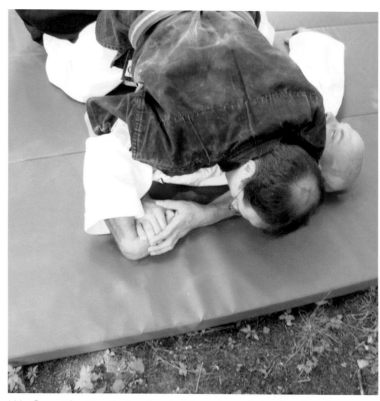

Ude Garami (position the head against the opponent's head and apply pressure to the wrist).

Ude Garami (interweave legs).

Ude Garami (attempt to straighten the legs).

Ude Hishigi Juji Gatame: Cross Arm-Lock

After throwing an opponent using Ippon Seio Nage (see Chapter 7) at the right side of the body, remain standing and slide your right hand up the opponent's right sleeve, grabbing onto the wrist or cuff at the end of his sleeve. Using both hands, pull upward on the opponent's right arm to lift his head slightly. Slide your left foot forward in order to insert the top of the left foot and the lower part of the left shin, thus positioning the side and back of the opponent's neck against the leg. Raise your right foot and move it along the right side of the opponent's arm and over his chest, gently positioning your heel onto the far side of the opponent's neck (as if to strike him with the heel), to secure it between your legs. Exert pressure on the opponent's neck by attempting to forcefully move your legs toward each other similar to a 'vice'. Continue to maintain upward pressure on the opponent's arm and drop to the rear, landing onto the Tatame. Keep the opponent's arm straight and position it sideways so the side of his elbow can be positioned against the inside of your right thigh. Pull the opponent's arm slowly to the right to apply gradual pressure to his elbow. Ude Hishigi Juji Gatame is performed using the opponent's left arm in a manner similar to that described using the opponent's right arm.

Ude Hishigi Juji Gatame (hold onto opponent).

Ude Hishigi Juji Gatame (pull arm upward).

Ude Hishigi Juji Gatame (position foot against the neck).

Ude Hishigi Juji Gatame (postion heel against the far side of the neck 1).

Ude Hishigi Juji Gatame (postion heel against the far side of the neck 2).

Ude Hishigi Juji Gatame (postion heel against the far side of the neck 3).

Ude Hishigi Juji Gatame (drop to rear).

Ude Hishigi Juji Gatame (keep opponent's arm straight).

Ude Hishigi Juji Gatame (apply pressure to elbow).

Ude Hishigi Juji Gatame (hold onto opponent).

Ude Hishigi Juji Gatame (pull arm upwards and positon foot against the neck).

Ude Hishigi Juji Gatame (postion heel against the far side of the neck 1).

Ude Hishigi Juji Gatame (postion heel against the far side of the neck 2).

Ude Hishigi Juji Gatame (apply pressure to elbow).

GLOSSARY

Aiki Ashi Kaiten Nage   Leg rotary throw.

Aiki Kote Gaeshi   Minor wrist overturn.

Aiki Morote Seio Nage   Two-handed shoulder throw.

Aiki Nage Waza   'Harmonizing energy' throws from sword and weapons-free attacks.

Aiki Sei Otoshi   Shoulder drop.

Aiki Soto Tekubi Nage   Outer wrist throw.

Aiki Tai Otoshi   Body drop.

Aiki Ude Kaiten Nage   Arm rotary throw.

Aiki Ura Shiho Nage   Circular four winds throw.

Aikido   The way of harmonizing energy.

Aiki-Jujutsu   Economical and subtle martial art of harmonizing energy.

Aiki-Jujutsu-Ka   Aiki-Jujutsu practitioner.

Aiki-Jutsu   Martial art of harmonizing energy.

Aiki-Ka   Aiki practitioner.

Aiki-Randori   Free-sparring in the Aiki arts.

Ashi Uke   Leg blocks.

Atemi Waza   Hand striking techniques.

Atemi   Strike.

Bokken   A wooden Samurai sword replica.

Budo   Martial ways.

Budo-Ka   Budo practitioner.

Bujutsu   Martial arts.

Bushi   Warrior.

Chuden Gyaku Tate Tsuki   Middle-level reverse vertical fist strike.

Chuden Oi Tate Tsuki   Middle-level vertical lunging fist strike.

Chuden Teisho Uke   Middle-level palm block.

Chuden Ude Ki Uke   Middle-level arm internal energy block.

Chuden   Middle-level.

Dachi Waza   Stances.

Daimyo   Lord or Samurai's master.

Dojo   Training hall.

Fukasa-Ryu   Profound martial arts style.

Gedan Barai Uke   Lower-level sweeping block.

Gedan Gyaku Kage Tsuki   Lower-level reverse hook strike.

Gedan Gyaku Tate Tsuki   Lower-level reverse vertical fist strike.

Gedan Oi Kage Tsuki   Lower-level lunging hook strike.

GLOSSARY

Gedan Oi Tate Tsuki Lower-level lunging vertical fist strike.

Gedan Te Uke Lower-level hand block.

Gedan Lower-level.

Geri Waza Kicking techniques.

Gi Uniform.

Gyaku Age Uchi, Aiki Tai Otoshi Body drop from reverse rising cut.

Gyaku Age Uchi Reverse diagonal rising cut.

Gyaku Juji Jime Reverse cross choke.

Gyaku Tsuki Reverse strikes.

Hadaka Jime Naked choke.

Hai Yes.

Hajame Begin.

Hakama Uniform skirt.

Hane Goshi Spring hip throw.

Hanmi Dachi Half-body stance.

Han-Sankyo Kneeling position with one knee touching the ground.

Hara Area of the body located around the lower abdominal cavity.

Harai Goshi Sweeping loin throw.

Hidari Left.

Hiji Ori Elbow break.

Hiza Uke Knee block.

Iai-Jutsu The art of drawing the Samurai sword most expeditiously.

Iai Mae Zempo Kaiten Front rotary roll with the sword.

Iie No.

Ippon Seio Nage One-arm shoulder throw.

Ippon Tai Sabaki Full body pivot.

Jigohontai Dachi Neutral stance.

Jigotai Dachi Defensive 'square' stance.

Jo Short staff measuring 4ft (1.2m) in length.

Joden Gyaku Kage Tsuki Upper-level reverse hook strike.

Joden Gyaku Tate Tsuki Upper-level reverse vertical fist strike.

Joden Kumai Upper-level sword guard position.

Joden Oi Kage Tsuki Upper-level lunging hook strike.

Joden Oi Tate Tsuki Upper-level lunging vertical fist strike.

Joden Teisho Uke Upper-level palm block.

Joden Ude Ki Uke Upper-level arm internal energy block.

Joden Upper-level.

Judo Gentle, efficient, soft way.

Judo-Ka Judo player/practitioner.

Ju-Jutsu Nage Waza Hip throws and sweeps.

Ju-Jutsu Soft, subtle, economical martial art.

Jujutsu Sometimes used interchangeably with Ju-Jutsu.

Ju-Jutsu-Ka Jujutsu practitioner.

Ka Practitioner.

Kansetsu Geri Joint kick.

Kansetsu Waza   Joint-locking techniques.

Kata   Forms or contrived sequences of movements.

Kata Gatame   Shoulder hold.

Kataha Gatame   Single wing lock.

Katame Waza   Groundwork 'holding' techniques.

Katana   Long Samurai sword.

Kempo-Jutsu   Fist law martial art.

Kempo-Jutsu-Ka   Kempo-Jutsu practitioner.

Ken-Jutsu   The art of fencing with the Samurai sword after it has been drawn.

Kesa Gatame   Scarf hold.

Ki   Internal energy.

Kio-Tsuke   Attention!

Kobudo   'Ancient martial ways' comprised of just one or a few martial arts that did not evolve over the course of many generations of Samurai service.

Kodokan   Famous Judo school (and Judo style) in Japan.

Kokutsu Dachi   Back stance.

Koryu   'Ancient martial Ryu' that proliferated during early Samurai times and evolved over the course of many generations of Samurai service.

Kosa Dachi   Cross stance.

Koshi Guruma   Hip wheel.

Kuzushi   Off-balancing techniques.

Mae Chugaeri   Front somersault break-fall.

Mae Kekomi Geri   Front thrust kick.

Mae Ukemi   Front break-fall.

Mae Zempo Kaiten   Front rotary roll.

Mawashi Geri   Roundhouse kick.

Migi   Right.

Mushin   'No-mindedness'.

Naginata   Glaive.

Nuki Dashi   Sword draw.

Nuki Dashi Age Rising   Oblique sword draw.

Nuki Dashi Tomoe   Stomach-level sword draw.

Nuki Dashi, Aiki Kote Gaeshi   Minor wrist overturn from a sword draw.

Nuki Dashi, Soto Tekubi Nage   Outer wrist throw from sword draw.

O Soto Gari   Major outer clip.

Obi   Belt.

Oi Kage Tsuki   Lunging hook strike.

Randori   Free-sparring.

Rei   Bow.

Reiken Uchi   Back knuckle strike.

Ryu   School of thought, style.

Saho   Formal etiquette.

Samurai   A servant that acted in the interests of his Daimyo (lord) and the country of Japan.

Seiken   Fist.

Seiza   Seated position.

Sempai   The most senior student.

Seppuku   Ritual suicide.

Shihan   A title given to a master level practitioner meaning 'one who points the way'.

Shikko Waza   Knee-walking techniques.

Shizentai Dachi   Natural stance.

Shogun   Military leader.

Shomen Uchi   Vertical downward head cut.

Shomen Uchi, Aiki Ashi Kaiten Nage   Leg rotary throw from vertical head cut.

Shomen Uchi, Aiki Morote Seio Nage   Two-handed shoulder throw from vertical head cut.

Shomen Uchi, Aiki Sei Otoshi   Shoulder drop from vertical head cut.

Shomen Uchi, Aiki Ura Shiho Nage   Circular four winds throw from vertical head cut.

Shuto Uchi   Knife hand strike.

Sode Tsuri Komi Goshi   Sleeve lift pull hip throw.

Tachi Dori   Sword disarming.

Tai Sabaki   Body pivots.

Tanto   Knife.

Tatame   Matted area.

Teisho Uke   Palm block.

Tomoe Nage   Stomach throw.

Tori   Thrower.

Tsuri Komi Goshi   Lift pull hip throw.

Tsuru Uke   Crane block.

Uchi Mata   Inner thigh throw.

Ude Garami   Arm entanglement.

Ude Gatame   Arm-lock.

Ude Hishigi Juji Gatame   Cross arm-lock.

Ude Ki Uke   Arm internal energy block.

Ude Osae Jime   Arm press choke.

Ue Tsuki   Upper-cut.

Uke Waza   Blocking techniques.

Ukemi Waza   Break-falling techniques.

Uki   Faller.

Uki Goshi   Minor hip throw.

Ushiro Kekomi Geri   Rear thrust kick.

Ushiro Ukemi   Rear break-fall.

Ushiro Zempo Kaiten   Rear rotary roll.

Uwagi   Uniform jacket.

Waza   Techniques.

Wazari Tai Sabaki   Half-body pivot.

Yari   Spear.

Yin & Yang   Offensive and defensive principles of attack.

Yoko Chugaeri   Side somersault break-fall.

Yoko Empi Uchi   Side elbow strike.

Yoko Kekomi Geri   Side thrust kick.

Yoko Ukemi   Side break-fall.

Zenkutsu Dachi   Forward 'locked-leg' stance.

INDEX

INDEX

RELATED TITLES FROM CROWOOD

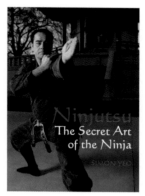

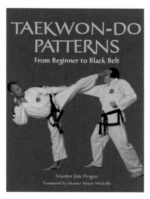
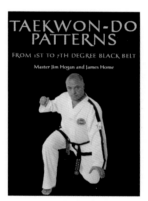